Machine Learning with scikit-learn Quick Start Guide

Classification, regression, and clustering techniques in Python

Kevin Jolly

BIRMINGHAM - MUMBAI

Machine Learning with scikit-learn Quick Start Guide

Copyright © 2018 Packt Publishing

Commissioning Editor: Amey Varangaonkar
Acquisition Editor: Aditi Gour
Content Development Editor: Smit Carvalho
Technical Editor: Jinesh Topiwala
Copy Editor: Safis Editing
Project Coordinator: Hardik Bhinde
Proofreader: Safis Editing
Indexer: Tejal Daruwale Soni
Graphics: Jason Monteiro
Production Coordinator: Jyoti Chauhan

First published: October 2018

Production reference: 2091118

Published by Packt Publishing Ltd.
Livery Place
35 Livery Street
Birmingham
B3 2PB, UK.

ISBN 978-1-78934-370-0

www.packtpub.com

To my parents for their unconditional support for all the choices I make.

– Kevin Jolly

`mapt.io`

Mapt is an online digital library that gives you full access to over 5,000 books and videos, as well as industry leading tools to help you plan your personal development and advance your career. For more information, please visit our website.

Why subscribe?

- Spend less time learning and more time coding with practical eBooks and Videos from over 4,000 industry professionals

- Improve your learning with Skill Plans built especially for you

- Get a free eBook or video every month

- Mapt is fully searchable

- Copy and paste, print, and bookmark content

Packt.com

Did you know that Packt offers eBook versions of every book published, with PDF and ePub files available? You can upgrade to the eBook version at `www.packt.com` and as a print book customer, you are entitled to a discount on the eBook copy. Get in touch with us at `customercare@packtpub.com` for more details.

At `www.packt.com`, you can also read a collection of free technical articles, sign up for a range of free newsletters, and receive exclusive discounts and offers on Packt books and eBooks.

Contributors

About the author

Kevin Jolly is a formally educated data scientist with a master's degree in data science from the prestigious King's College London. Kevin works as a statistical analyst with a digital healthcare start-up, Connido Limited, in London, where he is primarily involved in leading the data science projects that the company undertakes. He has built machine learning pipelines for small and big data, with a focus on scaling such pipelines into production for the products that the company has built.

Kevin is also the author of a book titled *Hands-On Data Visualization with Bokeh*, published by Packt. He is the editor-in-chief of Linear, a weekly online publication on data science software and products.

About the reviewers

Mehar Pratap Singh is one of the co-founders of ProCogia, and divides his time between their corporate headquarters in Vancouver, BC, and their Seattle office. Among his priorities is the marshaling of the diverse talents at ProCogia to expand the possibilities of data science and give their clients unbeatable competitive advantages.

Mehar was previously a data science consultant at T-Mobile, Microsoft, and several start-up ventures in Seattle. He holds an MBA from the University of Washington and an MS in electrical engineering from the University of Wisconsin.

Mehar's favorite party trick is to recite the entire chemical periodic table from memory. He is also an avid basketball player and loves following the NBA.

Joydeep Bhattacharjee is a principal engineer working for Nineleaps Technology Solutions. After graduating from the National Institute of Technology at Silchar, he started working in the software industry, where he stumbled upon Python. Through Python, he came across machine learning. Now he primarily develops intelligent systems that can parse and process data to solve challenging problems at work. He believes in sharing knowledge and loves mentoring in machine learning. He has published a book on FastText, a popular natural language processing tool, and loves speaking about machine learning at various national and international conferences.

Packt is searching for authors like you

If you're interested in becoming an author for Packt, please visit `authors.packtpub.com` and apply today. We have worked with thousands of developers and tech professionals, just like you, to help them share their insight with the global tech community. You can make a general application, apply for a specific hot topic that we are recruiting an author for, or submit your own idea.

Table of Contents

Preface

The fundamental aim of this book is help its readers quickly deploy, optimize, and evaluate every kind of machine learning algorithm that scikit-learn provides in an agile manner.

Readers will learn how to deploy supervised machine learning algorithms, such as logistic regression, k-nearest neighbors, linear regression, Support Vector Machines, Naive Bayes, and tree-based algorithms, in order to solve classification and regression machine learning problems.

Readers will also learn how to deploy unsupervised machine learning algorithms such as the k-means algorithm in order to cluster unlabeled data into groups.

Finally, readers will be provided with different techniques to visually interpret and evaluate the performance of the algorithms that they build.

Who this book is for

This book is for data scientists, software engineers, and people interested in machine learning with a background in Python who would like to understand, implement, and evaluate a wide range of machine learning algorithms using the scikit-learn framework.

What this book covers

Chapter 1, *Introducing Machine Learning with scikit-learn*, is a brief introduction to the different types of machine learning and its applications.

Chapter 2, *Predicting Categories with K-Nearest Neighbors*, covers working with and implementing the k-nearest neighbors algorithm to solve classification problems in scikit-learn.

Chapter 3, *Predicting Categories with Logistic Regression*, explains the workings and implementation of the logistic regression algorithm when solving classification problems in scikit-learn.

Chapter 4, *Predicting Categories with Naive Bayes and SVMs*, explains the workings and implementation of the Naive Bayes and the Linear Support Vector Machines algorithms when solving classification problems in scikit-learn.

Chapter 5, *Predicting Numeric Outcomes with Linear Regression*, explains the workings and implementation of the linear regression algorithm when solving regression problems in scikit-learn.

Chapter 6, *Classification and Regression with Trees*, explains the workings and implementation of tree-based algorithms such as decision trees, random forests, and the boosting and ensemble algorithms when solving classification and regression problems in scikit-learn.

Chapter 7, *Clustering Data with Unsupervised Machine Learning*, explains the workings and implementation of the k-means algorithm when solving unsupervised problems in scikit-learn.

Chapter 8, *Performance Evaluation Methods*, contains visual performance evaluation techniques for supervised and unsupervised machine learning algorithms.

To get the most out of this book

To get the most out of this book:

- Prior knowledge of Python is assumed at a basic level.
- Jupyter Notebook as a development environment is preferred but not necessary.

Download the example code files

You can download the example code files for this book from your account at www.packt.com. If you purchased this book elsewhere, you can visit www.packt.com/support and register to have the files emailed directly to you.

You can download the code files by following these steps:

1. Log in or register at www.packt.com.
2. Select the **SUPPORT** tab.
3. Click on **Code Downloads and Errata**.
4. Enter the name of the book in the **Search** box and follow the onscreen instructions.

Once the file is downloaded, please make sure that you unzip or extract the folder using the latest version of:

- WinRAR/7-Zip for Windows
- Zipeg/iZip/UnRarX for Mac
- 7-Zip/PeaZip for Linux

The code bundle for the book is also hosted on GitHub at `https://github.com/PacktPublishing/Machine-Learning-with-scikit-learn-Quick-Start-Guide`. In case there's an update to the code, it will be updated on the existing GitHub repository.

We also have other code bundles from our rich catalog of books and videos available at `https://github.com/PacktPublishing/`. Check them out!

Code in action

Visit the following link to check out videos of the code being run:
`http://bit.ly/2OcWIGH`

Conventions used

There are a number of text conventions used throughout this book.

`CodeInText`: Indicates code words in text, database table names, folder names, filenames, file extensions, pathnames, dummy URLs, user input, and Twitter handles. Here is an example: "Mount the downloaded `WebStorm-10*.dmg` disk image file as another disk in your system."

A block of code is set as follows:

```
from sklearn.naive_bayes import GaussianNB

#Initializing an NB classifier

nb_classifier = GaussianNB()

#Fitting the classifier into the training data

nb_classifier.fit(X_train, y_train)
```

```
#Extracting the accuracy score from the NB classifier

nb_classifier.score(X_test, y_test)
```

 Warnings or important notes appear like this.

 Tips and tricks appear like this.

Get in touch

Feedback from our readers is always welcome.

General feedback: If you have questions about any aspect of this book, mention the book title in the subject of your message and email us at customercare@packtpub.com.

Errata: Although we have taken every care to ensure the accuracy of our content, mistakes do happen. If you have found a mistake in this book, we would be grateful if you would report this to us. Please visit www.packt.com/submit-errata, selecting your book, clicking on the Errata Submission Form link, and entering the details.

Piracy: If you come across any illegal copies of our works in any form on the Internet, we would be grateful if you would provide us with the location address or website name. Please contact us at copyright@packt.com with a link to the material.

If you are interested in becoming an author: If there is a topic that you have expertise in and you are interested in either writing or contributing to a book, please visit authors.packtpub.com.

Reviews

Please leave a review. Once you have read and used this book, why not leave a review on the site that you purchased it from? Potential readers can then see and use your unbiased opinion to make purchase decisions, we at Packt can understand what you think about our products, and our authors can see your feedback on their book. Thank you!

For more information about Packt, please visit packt.com.

Introducing Machine Learning with scikit-learn

1

Welcome to the world of machine learning with scikit-learn. I'm thrilled that you have chosen this book in order to begin or further advance your knowledge on the vast field of machine learning. Machine learning can be overwhelming at times and this is partly due to the large number of tools that are available on the market. This book will simplify this process of tool selection down to one – scikit-learn.

If I were to tell you what this book can do for you in one sentence, it would be this – *The book gives you pipelines that can be implemented in order to solve a wide range of machine learning problems.* True to what this sentence implies, you will learn how to construct an end-to-end machine learning pipeline using some of the most popular algorithms that are widely used in the industry and professional competitions, such as Kaggle.

However, in this introductory chapter, we will go through the following topics:

- A brief introduction to machine learning
- What is scikit-learn?
- Installing scikit-learn
- Algorithms that you will learn to implement scikit-learn in this book

Now, let's begin this fun journey into the world of machine learning with scikit-learn!

A brief introduction to machine learning

Machine learning has generated quite the buzz – from Elon Musk fearing the role of unregulated artificial intelligence in society, to Mark Zuckerberg having a view that contradicts Musk's.

So, what exactly is machine learning? Simply put, machine learning is a set of **methods** that can detect patterns in data and use those patterns to make future predictions. Machine learning has found immense value in a wide range of industries, ranging from finance to healthcare. This translates to a higher requirement of talent with the skill capital in the field of machine learning.

Broadly speaking, machine learning can be categorized into three main types:

- Supervised learning
- Unsupervised learning
- Reinforcement learning

Scikit-learn is designed to tackle problems pertaining to supervised and unsupervised learning only, and does not support reinforcement learning at present.

Supervised learning

Supervised learning is a form of machine learning in which our data comes with a set of labels or a target variable that is numeric. These labels/categories usually belong to one feature/attribute, which is commonly known as the **target variable.** For instance, each row of your data could either belong to the category of *Healthy* or *Not Healthy*.

Given a set of features such as weight, blood sugar levels, and age, we can use the supervised machine learning algorithm to predict whether the person is healthy or not.

In the following simple mathematical expression, **S** is the supervised learning algorithm, **X** is the set of input features, such as weight and age, and **Y** is the target variable with the labels *Healthy* or *Not Healthy*:

$$S = [X,Y]$$

Although supervised machine learning is the most common type of machine learning that is implemented with scikit-learn and in the industry, most datasets typically do not come with predefined labels. Unsupervised learning algorithms are first used to cluster data without labels into distinct groups to which we can then assign labels. This is discussed in detail in the following section.

Unsupervised learning

Unsupervised learning is a form of machine learning in which the algorithm tries to detect/find patterns in data that do not have an outcome/target variable. In other words, we do not have data that comes with pre-existing labels. Thus, the algorithm will typically use a metric such as distance to group data together depending on how close they are to each other.

As discussed in the previous section, most of the data that you will encounter in the real world will not come with a set of predefined labels and, as such, will only have a set of input features without a target attribute.

In the following simple mathematical expression, **U** is the unsupervised learning algorithm, while **X** is a set of input features, such as weight and age:

$$U = [X]$$

Given this data, our objective is to create groups that could potentially be labeled as *Healthy* or *Not Healthy*. The unsupervised learning algorithm will use a metric such as distance in order to identify how close a set of points are to each other and how far apart two such groups are. The algorithm will then proceed to cluster these groups into two distinct groups, as illustrated in the following diagram:

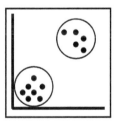

Clustering two groups together

What is scikit-learn?

Scikit-learn is a free and open source software that helps you tackle supervised and unsupervised machine learning problems. The software is built entirely in Python and utilizes some of the most popular libraries that Python has to offer, namely NumPy and SciPy.

The main reason why scikit-learn is very popular stems from the fact that most of the world's most popular machine learning algorithms can be implemented quite quickly in a plug and play format once you know what the core pipeline is like. Another reason is that popular algorithms for classification such as **logistic regression** and **support vector machines** are written in Cython. Cython is used to give these algorithms *C-like* performance and thus makes the use of scikit-learn quite efficient in the process.

Installing scikit-learn

There are two ways in which you can install scikit-learn on your personal device:

- By using the pip method
- By using the Anaconda method

The pip method can be implemented on the macOS/Linux Terminal or the Windows PowerShell, while the Anaconda method will work with the Anaconda prompt.

Choosing between these two methods of installation is pretty straightforward:

- If you would like all the common Python package distributions for data science to be installed in one environment, the Anaconda method works best
- If you would like to build you own environment from scratch for scikit-learn, the pip method works best (for advanced users of Python)

 This book will be using Python 3.6 for all the code that is displayed throughout every chapter, unless mentioned otherwise.

The pip method

Scikit-learn requires a few packages to be installed on your device before you can install it. These are as follows:

- **NumPy**: Version 1.8.2 or greater
- **SciPy**: Version 0.13.3 or greater

These can be installed using the pip method by using the following commands:

```
pip3 install NumPy
```

```
pip3 install SciPy
```

Next, we can install scikit-learn using the following code:

```
pip3 install scikit-learn
```

Additionally, if you already have scikit-learn installed on your device and you simply want to upgrade it to the latest version, you can use the following code:

```
pip3 install -U scikit-learn
```

The version of scikit-learn implemented in the book is 0.19.1.

The Anaconda method

In the event that you have installed Python using the Anaconda distribution, you can install scikit-learn by using the following code in the Anaconda prompt:

The first step is to install the dependencies:

```
conda install NumPy
```

```
conda install SciPy
```

Next, we can install scikit-learn by using the following code:

```
conda install scikit-learn
```

Additionally, if you already have scikit-learn installed with the Anaconda distribution, you can upgrade it to the latest version by using the following code in the Anaconda prompt:

```
conda update scikit-learn
```

When upgrading or uninstalling scikit-learn that has been installed with Anaconda, avoid using the pip method at all costs as doing so is most likely going to fail upgrading or removing all the required files. Stick with either the pip method or the Anaconda method in order to maintain consistency.

Additional packages

In this section, we will talk about the packages that we will be installing outside of scikit-learn that will be used throughout this book.

Pandas

To install Pandas, you can use either the pip method or the Anaconda method, as follows:

Pip method:

```
pip3 install pandas
```

Anaconda method:

```
conda install pandas
```

Matplotlib

To install matplotlib, you can use either the pip method or the Anaconda method, as follows:

Pip method:

```
pip3 install matplotlib
```

Anaconda method:

```
conda install matplotlib
```

Tree

To install tree, you can use either the pip method or the Anaconda method, as follows:

Pip method:

```
pip3 install tree
```

Anaconda method:

```
conda install tree
```

Pydotplus

To install pydotplus, you can use either the pip method or the Anaconda method, as follows:

Pip method:

```
pip3 install pydotplus
```

Anaconda method:

```
conda install pydotplus
```

Image

To install Image, you can use either the pip method or the Anaconda method, as follows:

Pip method:

```
pip3 install Image
```

Anaconda method:

```
conda install Image
```

Algorithms that you will learn to implement using scikit-learn

The algorithms that you will learn about in this book are broadly classified into the following two categories:

- Supervised learning algorithms
- Unsupervised learning algorithms

Supervised learning algorithms

Supervised learning algorithms can be used to solve both classification and regression problems. In this book, you will learn how to implement some of the most popular supervised machine learning algorithms. Popular supervised machine learning algorithms are the ones that are widely used in industry and research, and have helped us solve a wide range of problems across a wide range of domains. These supervised learning algorithms are as follows:

- **Linear regression**: This supervised learning algorithm is used to predict continuous numeric outcomes such as house prices, stock prices, and temperature, to name a few
- **Logistic regression**: The logistic learning algorithm is a popular classification algorithm that is especially used in the credit industry in order to predict loan defaults
- **k-Nearest Neighbors**: The k-NN algorithm is a classification algorithm that is used to classify data into two or more categories, and is widely used to classify houses into expensive and affordable categories based on price, area, bedrooms, and a whole range of other features
- **Support vector machines**: The SVM algorithm is a popular classification algorithm that is used in image and face detection, along with applications such as handwriting recognition
- **Tree-Based algorithms:** Tree-based algorithms such as decision trees, Random Forests, and Boosted trees are used to solve both classification and regression problems
- **Naive Bayes:** The Naive Bayes classifier is a machine learning algorithm that uses the mathematical model of probability to solve classification problems

Unsupervised learning algorithms

Unsupervised machine learning algorithms are typically used to cluster points of data based on distance. The unsupervised learning algorithm that you will learn about in this book is as follows:

- **k-means**: The k-means algorithm is a popular algorithm that is typically used to segment customers into unique categories based on a variety of features, such as their spending habits. This algorithm is also used to segment houses into categories based on their features, such as price and area.

Summary

This chapter has given you a brief introduction into what machine learning is for those of you who are just beginning your journey into the world of machine learning. You have learned about how scikit-learn fits into the context of machine learning and how you can go about installing the necessary software.

Finally, you had a brief glimpse at all the algorithms that you will learn to implement as you progress through this book, as well as its associated applications in the real world.

In the next chapter, you will learn how to implement your first algorithm – the K-Nearest Neighbors algorithm!

Predicting Categories with K-Nearest Neighbors 2

The **k-Nearest Neighbors** (**k-NN**) algorithm is a form of supervised machine learning that is used to predict categories. In this chapter, you will learn about the following:

- Preparing a dataset for machine learning with scikit-learn
- How the k-NN algorithm works *under the hood*
- Implementing your first k-NN algorithm to predict a fraudulent transaction
- Fine-tuning the parameters of the k-NN algorithm
- Scaling your data for optimized performance

The k-NN algorithm has a wide range of applications in the field of classification and supervised machine learning. Some of the real-world applications for this algorithm include predicting loan defaults and credit-based fraud in the financial industry and predicting whether a patient has cancer in the healthcare industry.

This book's design facilitates the implementation of a robust machine learning pipeline for each and every algorithm mentioned in the book, and a Jupyter Notebook will be required.

The Jupyter Notebook can be installed on your local machine by following the instructions provided at: `https://jupyter.org/install.html`.

Alternatively, you can also work with the Jupyter Notebook in the browser by using: `https://jupyter.org/try`.

 Each chapter in this book comes with a pipeline that is implemented in a Jupyter Notebook on the official GitHub repository of this book, and as such, it is highly recommended that you install Jupyter Notebook on your local machine.

Technical requirements

You will be required to have Python 3.6 or greater, Pandas ≥ 0.23.4, Scikit-learn ≥ 0.20.0, NumPy ≥ 1.15.1, and Matplotlib ≥ 3.0.0 installed on your system.

The code files of this chapter can be found on GitHub:
`https://github.com/PacktPublishing/Machine-Learning-with-scikit-learn-Quick-Start-Guide/blob/master/Chapter_02.ipynb`

Check out the following video to see the code in action:

`http://bit.ly/2Q2DGop`

Preparing a dataset for machine learning with scikit-learn

The first step to implementing any machine learning algorithm with scikit-learn is data preparation. Scikit-learn comes with a set of constraints to implementation that will be discussed later in this section. The dataset that we will be using is based on mobile payments and is found on the world's most popular competitive machine learning website – Kaggle.

You can download the dataset from: `https://www.kaggle.com/ntnu-testimon/paysim1`.

Once downloaded, open a new Jupyter Notebook by using the following code in Terminal (macOS/Linux) or Anaconda Prompt/PowerShell (Windows):

```
Jupyter Notebook
```

The fundamental goal of this dataset is to predict whether a mobile transaction is fraudulent. In order to do this, we need to first have a brief understanding of the contents of our data. In order to explore the dataset, we will use the `pandas` package in Python. You can install pandas by using the following code in Terminal (macOS/Linux) or PowerShell (Windows):

```
pip3 install pandas
```

Pandas can be installed on Windows machines in an Anaconda Prompt by using the following code:

```
conda install pandas
```

We can now read in the dataset into our Jupyter Notebook by using the following code:

```
#Package Imports

import pandas as pd

#Reading in the dataset

df = pd.read_csv('PS_20174392719_1491204439457_log.csv')

#Viewing the first 5 rows of the dataset

df.head()
```

This produces an output as illustrated in the following screenshot:

step	type	amount	nameOrig	oldbalanceOrg	newbalanceOrig	nameDest	oldbalanceDest	newbalanceDest	isFraud	isFlaggedFraud
1	PAYMENT	9839.64	C1231006815	170136.0	160296.36	M1979787155	0.0	0.0	0	0
1	PAYMENT	1864.28	C1666544295	21249.0	19384.72	M2044282225	0.0	0.0	0	0
1	TRANSFER	181.00	C1305486145	181.0	0.00	C553264065	0.0	0.0	1	0
1	CASH_OUT	181.00	C840083671	181.0	0.00	C38997010	21182.0	0.0	1	0
1	PAYMENT	11668.14	C2048537720	41554.0	29885.86	M1230701703	0.0	0.0	0	0

Dropping features that are redundant

From the dataset seen previously, there are a few columns that are redundant to the machine learning process:

- `nameOrig`: This column is a unique identifier that belongs to each customer. Since each identifier is unique with every row of the dataset, the machine learning algorithm will not be able to discern any patterns from this feature.
- `nameDest`: This column is also a unique identifier that belongs to each customer and as such provides no value to the machine learning algorithm.
- `isFlaggedFraud`: This column flags a transaction as fraudulent if a person tries to transfer more than 200,000 in a single transaction. Since we already have a feature called `isFraud` that flags a transaction as fraud, this feature becomes redundant.

We can drop these features from the dataset by using the following code:

```
#Dropping the redundant features

df = df.drop(['nameOrig', 'nameDest', 'isFlaggedFraud'], axis = 1)
```

Reducing the size of the data

The dataset that we are working with contains over 6 million rows of data. Most machine learning algorithms will take a large amount of time to work with a dataset of this size. In order to make our execution time quicker, we will reduce the size of the dataset to 20,000 rows. We can do this by using the following code:

```
#Storing the fraudulent data into a dataframe

df_fraud = df[df['isFraud'] == 1]

#Storing the non-fraudulent data into a dataframe

df_nofraud = df[df['isFraud'] == 0]

#Storing 12,000 rows of non-fraudulent data

df_nofraud = df_nofraud.head(12000)

#Joining both datasets together

df = pd.concat([df_fraud, df_nofraud], axis = 0)
```

In the preceding code, the fraudulent rows are stored in one dataframe. This dataframe contains a little over 8,000 rows. The 12,000 non-fraudulent rows are stored in another dataframe, and the two dataframes are joined together using the concat method from pandas.

This results in a dataframe with a little over 20,000 rows, over which we can now execute our algorithms relatively quickly.

Encoding the categorical variables

One of the main constraints of scikit-learn is that you cannot implement the machine learning algorithms on columns that are categorical in nature. For example, the type column in our dataset has five categories:

- CASH-IN
- CASH-OUT
- DEBIT
- PAYMENT
- TRANSFER

These categories will have to be encoded into numbers that scikit-learn can make sense of. In order to do this, we have to implement a two-step process.

The first step is to convert each category into a number: CASH-IN = 0, CASH-OUT = 1, DEBIT = 2, PAYMENT = 3, TRANSFER = 4. We can do this by using the following code:

```
#Package Imports

from sklearn.preprocessing import LabelEncoder
from sklearn.preprocessing import OneHotEncoder

#Converting the type column to categorical

df['type'] = df['type'].astype('category')

#Integer Encoding the 'type' column

type_encode = LabelEncoder()

#Integer encoding the 'type' column

df['type'] = type_encode.fit_transform(df.type)
```

The code first coverts the type column to a categorical feature. We then use LabelEncoder() in order to initialize an integer encoder object that is called type_encode. Finally, we apply the fit_transform method on the type column in order to convert each category into a number.

Broadly speaking, there are two types of categorical variables:

- Nominal
- Ordinal

Nominal categorical variables have no inherent order to them. An example of the nominal type of categorical variable is the type column.

Ordinal categorical variables have an inherent order to them. An example of the ordinal type of categorical variable is Education Level, in which people with a Master's degree will have a higher order/value compared to people with a Undergraduate degree only.

In the case of ordinal categorical variables, integer encoding, as illustrated previously, is sufficient and we do not need to one-hot encode them. Since the `type` column is a nominal categorical variable, we have to one-hot encode it after integer encoding it. This is done by using the following code:

```
#One hot encoding the 'type' column

type_one_hot = OneHotEncoder()

type_one_hot_encode =
type_one_hot.fit_transform(df.type.values.reshape(-1,1)).toarray()

#Adding the one hot encoded variables to the dataset

ohe_variable = pd.DataFrame(type_one_hot_encode, columns =
["type_"+str(int(i)) for i in range(type_one_hot_encode.shape[1])])

df = pd.concat([df, ohe_variable], axis=1)

#Dropping the original type variable

df = df.drop('type', axis = 1)

#Viewing the new dataframe after one-hot-encoding

df.head()
```

In the code, we first create a one-hot encoding object called `type_one_hot`. We then transform the `type` column into one-hot encoded columns by using the `fit_transform` method.

We have five categories that are represented by integers 0 to 4. Each of these five categories will now get its own column. Therefore, we create five columns called `type_0`, `type_1`, `type_2`, `type_3`, and `type_4`. Each of these five columns is represented by two values: 1, which indicates the presence of that category, and 0, which indicates the absence of that category.

This information is stored in the `ohe_variable`. Since this variable holds the five columns, we will join this to the original dataframe by using the `concat` method from `pandas`.

The ordinal `type` column is then dropped from the dataframe as this column is now redundant post one hot encoding. The final dataframe now looks like this:

	step	amount	oldbalanceOrg	newbalanceOrig	oldbalanceDest	newbalanceDest	isFraud	type_0	type_1	type_2	type_3	type_4
0	1.0	9839.64	170136.0	160296.36	0.0	0.0	0.0	0.0	0.0	0.0	0.0	1.0
1	1.0	1864.28	21249.0	19384.72	0.0	0.0	0.0	0.0	1.0	0.0	0.0	0.0
2	1.0	181.00	181.0	0.00	0.0	0.0	1.0	0.0	0.0	0.0	0.0	1.0
3	1.0	181.00	181.0	0.00	21182.0	0.0	1.0	0.0	1.0	0.0	0.0	0.0
4	1.0	11668.14	41554.0	29885.86	0.0	0.0	0.0	0.0	0.0	0.0	0.0	1.0

Missing values

Another constraint with scikit-learn is that it cannot handle data with missing values. Therefore, we must check whether our dataset has any missing values in any of the columns to begin with. We can do this by using the following code:

```
#Checking every column for missing values

df.isnull().any()
```

This produces this output:

```
step              True
type              True
amount            True
oldbalanceOrg     True
newbalanceOrig    True
oldbalanceDest    True
newbalanceDest    True
isFraud           True
type_0            True
type_1            True
type_2            True
type_3            True
type_4            True
dtype: bool
```

Here we note that every column has some amount of missing values.

Missing values can be handled in a variety of ways, such as the following:

- Median imputation
- Mean imputation
- Filling them with the majority value

The amount of techniques is quite large and varies depending on the nature of your dataset. This process of handling features with missing values is called **feature engineering**.

Feature engineering can be done for both categorical and numerical columns and would require an entire book to explain the various methodologies that comprise the topic.

Since this book provides you with a deep focus on the art of applying the various machine learning algorithms that scikit-learn offers, feature engineering will not be dealt with.

So, for the purpose of aligning with the goals that this book intends to achieve, we will impute all the missing values with a zero.

We can do this by using the following code:

```
#Imputing the missing values with a 0

df = df.fillna(0)
```

We now have a dataset that is ready for machine learning with scikit-learn. We will use this dataset for all the other chapters that we will go through in the future. To make it easy for us, then, we will export this dataset as a .csv file and store it in the same directory that you are working in with the Jupyter Notebook.

We can do this by using the following code:

```
df.to_csv('fraud_prediction.csv')
```

This will create a .csv file of this dataset in the directory that you are working in, which you can load into the notebook again using pandas.

The k-NN algorithm

Mathematically speaking, the k-NN algorithm is one of the most simple machine learning algorithms out there. See the following diagram for a visual overview of how it works:

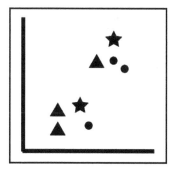

How k-NN works under the hood

The stars in the preceding diagram represent new data points. If we built a k-NN algorithm with three neighbors, then the stars would search for the three data points that are closest to it.

In the lower-left case, the star sees two triangles and one circle. Therefore, the algorithm would classify the star as a triangle since the number of triangles was greater than the number of circles.

In the upper-right case, the star sees two circles and one circle. Therefore, the algorithm will classify the star as a circle since the number of circles was greater than the number of triangles.

The real algorithm does this in a very probabilistic manner and picks the category/shape with the highest probability.

Implementing the k-NN algorithm using scikit-learn

In the following section, we will implement the first version of the k-NN algorithm and assess its initial accuracy. When implementing machine learning algorithms using scikit-learn, it is always a good practice to implement algorithms without fine-tuning or optimizing any of the associated parameters first in order to evaluate how well it performs.

In the following section, you will learn how to do the following:

- Split your data into training and test sets
- Implement the first version of the algorithm on the data
- Evaluate the accuracy of your model using a k-NN score

Splitting the data into training and test sets

The idea of training and test sets is fundamental to every machine learning problem. When thinking about this concept, it is easy to understand why the concept was introduced. Think of machine learning as the direct equivalent to the process of human learning; when learning a concept in mathematics, we first learn how to solve a set of problems with solutions attached to them so that we can understand the exact methodology involved in solving these problems. We then take a test at school or university and attempt to solve problems that we have not encountered or seen before in order to test our understanding.

The training set is a part of the dataset that a machine learning algorithm uses to learn from. The test set is a part of the dataset that the machine learning algorithm has not seen before and is used to assess the performance of the machine learning algorithm.

The first step to this process is to save all our features into one variable and the target variable, which contains the labels into another variable.

In our dataset, the target variable is called `isFraud` and contains two labels: 0 if the transaction is not a fraud and 1 if the transaction is a fraud. The features are the remaining variables. We can store these into two separate variables by using the following code:

```
#Creating the features

features = df.drop('isFraud', axis = 1).values
target = df['isFraud'].values
```

In the preceding code, *.values* is used to convert the values in the features and target variables into NumPy arrays.

Next, we will split the features and target into training and test sets by using the following code:

```
from sklearn.model_selection import train_test_split

X_train, X_test, y_train, y_test = train_test_split(features, target,
test_size = 0.3, random_state = 42, stratify = target)
```

We use the `train_test_split` from `sklearn.model_selection` in order to perform this task. In the preceding code, we have four variables. `X_train` and `X_test` correspond to the training and test sets for the features, while `y_train` and `y_test` correspond to training and test sets for the target variable.

The `train_test_split()` function takes in four arguments. The first argument is the array containing the features, the second argument is the array containing the target variable. The `test_size` argument is used to specify the amount of data that will be split and stored into the test set. Since we specified 0.3, 30% of the original data will be stored in the test set, while 70% of the original data will be used for training.

There are two primary ways in which the `train_test_split()` function shuffles data into training and test sets for the target variable:

- **Random sampling**: Randomly puts target labels into training and test sets (`y_train` and `y_test` in the preceding case).
- **Stratified sampling**: Ensures that the target labels are represented adequately in the training and test sets. In the preceding code, the *stratify* argument has been set to the target labels to ensure that this happens.

Implementation and evaluation of your model

Now that we have the training and test splits, we can implement the k-NN algorithm on the training sets and evaluate its score on the test sets. We can do this by using the following code:

```
from sklearn.neighbors import KNeighborsClassifier

#Initializing the kNN classifier with 3 neighbors

knn_classifier = KNeighborsClassifier(n_neighbors=3)

#Fitting the classifier on the training data

knn_classifier.fit(X_train, y_train)

#Extracting the accuracy score from the test sets

knn_classifier.score(X_test, y_test)
```

In the preceding code, we first initialize a k-NN classifier with three neighbors. The number of neighbors is chosen arbitrarily, and three is a good starting number. Next, we use the `.fit()` method to fit this classifier onto our training data. Finally, by using the `.score()` method on the test data, we obtain a value between 0 and 1 that indicates how accurate the classifier is.

In our case, we obtained an accuracy score of 0.98, which is very good!

There are many ways of assessing and evaluating the performance of the classifier, and the accuracy score should not be the only way you evaluate the performance of your classifier. Further methods of evaluation will be discussed at a later stage in the chapter.

Fine-tuning the parameters of the k-NN algorithm

In the previous section, we arbitrarily set the number of neighbors to three while initializing the k-NN classifier. However, is this the optimal value? Well, it could be, since we obtained a relatively high accuracy score in the test set.

Our goal is to create a machine learning model that does not overfit or underfit the data. Overfitting the data means that the model has been trained very specifically to the training examples provided and will not generalize well to cases/examples of data that it has not encountered before. For instance, we might have fit the model very specifically to the training data, with the test cases being also very similar to the training data. Thus, the model would have been able to perform very well and produce a very high value of accuracy.

Underfitting is another extreme case, in which the model fits the data in a very generic way and does not perform well in predicting the correct class labels in the test set. This is the exact opposite of overfitting.

Both these cases can be avoided by visualizing how well the model performs in the training and test sets by using a different number of neighbors. To do this, we first find the optimal number of neighbors by using the GridSearchCV algorithm.

GridSearchCV creates an empty grid and fills it with possible values of the number of neighbors or any other machine learning parameter that we want to optimize. It then uses each value in the grid and tests its performance and determines the optimal value of the parameter. We can implement the GridSearchCV algorithm to find the optimal number of neighbors by using the following code:

```
import numpy as np
from sklearn.model_selection import GridSearchCV

#Initializing a grid with possible number of neighbors from 1 to 24

grid = {'n_neighbors' : np.arange(1, 25)}

#Initializing a k-NN classifier
```

```
knn_classifier = KNeighborsClassifier()

#Using cross validation to find optimal number of neighbors

knn = GridSearchCV(knn_classifier, grid, cv = 10)

knn.fit(X_train, y_train)

#Extracting the optimal number of neighbors

knn.best_params_

#Extracting the accuracy score for optimal number of neighbors

knn.best_score_
```

In this code, we first initialize a number array with values between 1 and 24. This range was chosen arbitrarily and you can increase or decrease the range. However, increasing the range will mean that it will take more computational time to compute and find the optimal number of neighbors, especially when your dataset is large.

Next, we initialize a k-NN classifier and use the `GridSearchCV()` function on the classifier along with the grid. We set the `cv` argument to 10, indicating that we want to use 10-fold cross validation while doing this. Cross validation is a technique in which the classifier first divides the data into 10 parts. The first nine parts are used as the training set while the 10th part is used as the test set. In the second iteration, we use the first eight parts and the 10th part as the training set, while the ninth part is used as the test set. This process is repeated until every part of the data is used for testing. This creates a very robust classifier, since we have used the entire dataset for training and testing and have not left out any part of the data.

Cross-validation is illustrated for you in the following diagram:

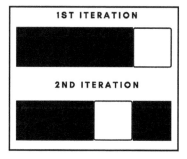

Cross-validation in action

In the preceding diagram, the black boxes illustrate the training data while the white box illustrates the test data.

Finally, we use the .best_params_ to extract the optimal number of neighbors. In our case, the optimal number of neighbors was 1, which resulted in an accuracy score of 0.985. This is an improvement of 0.002 from the original classifier that we built, which had a score of 0.983 with three neighbors.

Using cross-validation ensures that we do not overfit or underfit the data as we have used the entire dataset for training and testing.

Scaling for optimized performance

The k-NN algorithm is an algorithm that works based on distance. When a new data point is thrown into the dataset and the algorithm is given the task of classifying this new data point, it uses distance to check the points that are closest to it.

If we have features that have different ranges of values – for example, feature one has a range between 0 to 800 while feature two has a range between one to five – this distance metric does not make sense anymore. We want all the features to have the same range of values so that the distance metric is on level terms across all features.

One way to do this is to subtract each value of each feature by the mean of that feature and divide by the variance of that feature. This is called **standardization**:

$$Standardization = (RowValue - Meanacrossallvaluesof Feature)/Varianceacrossallvaluesof Feature$$

We can do this for our dataset by using the following code:

```
from sklearn.preprocessing import StandardScaler
from sklearn.pipeline import Pipeline

#Setting up the scaling pipeline

pipeline_order = [('scaler', StandardScaler()), ('knn',
KNeighborsClassifier(n_neighbors = 1))]

pipeline = Pipeline(pipeline_order)

#Fitting the classfier to the scaled dataset

knn_classifier_scaled = pipeline.fit(X_train, y_train)
```

```
#Extracting the score

knn_classifier_scaled.score(X_test, y_test)
```

In this code, we specify the order in which the pipeline has to be executed. We store this order in a variable called `pipeline_order` by specifying that we want to scale our data first by using the `StandardScaler()` function and then build a k-NN classifier with one neighbor.

Next, we use the `Pipeline()` function and pass in the order of the pipeline as the only argument. We then fit this pipeline to the training set and extract the accuracy scores from the test set.

The `Pipeline` function, as the name implies, is used to fit multiple functions into a pipeline and execute them in a specified order that we think is apt for the process. This function helps us streamline and automate common machine learning tasks.

This resulted in an accuracy score of `0.997`, which is a substantial improvement from the score of `0.985`. Thus, we see how scaling the data results in improved performance.

Summary

This chapter was fundamental in helping you prepare a dataset for machine learning with scikit-learn. You have learned about the constraints that are imposed when you do machine learning with scikit-learn and how to create a dataset that is perfect for scikit-learn.

You have also learned how the k-NN algorithm works behind the scenes and have implemented a version of it using scikit-learn to predict whether a transaction was fraudulent. You then learned how to optimize the parameters of the algorithm using the popular `GridSearchCV` algorithm. Finally, you have learnt how to standardize and scale your data in order to optimize the performance of your model.

In the next chapter, you will learn how to classify fraudulent transactions yet again with a new algorithm – the logistic regression algorithm!

3
Predicting Categories with Logistic Regression

The logistic regression algorithm is one of the most interpretable algorithms in the world of machine learning, and although the word "regression" implies predicting a numerical outcome, the logistic regression algorithm is, used to predict categories and solve classification machine learning problems.

In this chapter, you will learn about the following:

- How the logistic regression algorithm works mathematically
- Implementing and evaluating your first logistic regression algorithm with scikit-learn
- Fine-tuning the hyperparameters using `GridSearchCV`
- Scaling your data for a potential improvement in accuracy
- Interpreting the results of the model

Logistic regression has a wide range of applications, especially in the field of finance, where building interpretable machine learning models is key in convincing both investors and regulators alike that your model makes intuitive and logical sense.

Technical requirements

You will be required to have Python 3.6 or greater, Pandas ≥ 0.23.4, Scikit-learn ≥ 0.20.0, and Matplotlib ≥ 3.0.0 installed on your system.

The code files of this chapter can be found on GitHub:
https://github.com/PacktPublishing/Machine-Learning-with-scikit-learn-Quick-Start-Guide/blob/master/Chapter_03.ipynb

Check out the following video to see the code in action:

```
http://bit.ly/2DaTNgQ
```

Understanding logistic regression mathematically

As the name implies, logistic regression is fundamentally derived from the linear regression algorithm. The linear regression algorithm will be discussed in depth in the upcoming chapters. For now, let's consider a hypothetical case in which we want to predict the probability that a particular loan will default based on the loan's interest rate. Using linear regression, the following equation can be constructed:

```
Default = (Interest Rate × x) + c
```

In the preceding equation, c is the intercept and x is a coefficient that will be the output from the logistic regression model. The intercept and the coefficient will have numeric values. For the purpose of this example, let's assume c is 5 and x is -0.2. The equation now becomes this:

```
Default = (Interest Rate × -0.2) + 5
```

The equation can be represented in a two-dimensional plot using the following diagram:

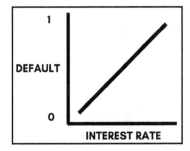

Assuming that the interest rate is 10%, the value of default produced by the equation is as follows:

$$Default = (10 × -0.2) + 5$$

$$Default = 3$$

The logistic regression model now uses the `logit` function to transform this value of 3 into a probability between 0 and 1:

$$\frac{1}{1 + e^-3}$$

After evaluating the preceding equation, we get an answer of 0.95. In other words, using the logistic regression model that we just built mathematically, we obtained a probability of 95% that the loan would default if the interest rate was 10%.

After applying the `logit` function to the linear equation, the two-dimensional plot shown previously changes to the following diagram:

In the preceding diagram, the following is happening:

- The function approaches 1 as the interest rate nears infinity along the *x*-axis.
- The function approaches 0 as the interest rate nears 0 along the *x*-axis.

Implementing logistic regression using scikit-learn

In this section, you will learn how you can implement and quickly evaluate a logistic regression model for your dataset. We will be using the same dataset that we have already cleaned and prepared for the purpose of predicting whether a particular transaction was fraudulent. In the previous chapter, we saved this dataset as `fraud_detection.csv`. The first step is to load this dataset into your Jupyter Notebook. This can be done by using the following code:

```
import pandas as pd

# Reading in the dataset

df = pd.read_csv('fraud_prediction.csv')
```

Splitting the data into training and test sets

The first step to building any machine learning model with scikit-learn is to split the data into training and test sets. This can be done by using the following code:

```
from sklearn.model_selection import train_test_split

#Creating the features and target

features = df.drop('isFraud', axis = 1).values
target = df['isFraud'].values

#Creating the training and testing data

X_train, X_test, y_train, y_test = train_test_split(features, target,
test_size = 0.3, random_state = 42, stratify = target)
```

The next step is to implement a base logistic regression classifier and evaluate its accuracy score. This can be done by using the following code:

```
from sklearn import linear_model

#Initializing an logistic regression object

logistic_regression = linear_model.LogisticRegression()

#Fitting the model to the training and test sets

logistic_regression.fit(X_train, y_train)
```

In the preceding code, the `linear_model` package is imported from `sklearn` and is used to initialize the logistic regression algorithm by calling the `LogisticRegression()` method. This logistic regression algorithm is then fit into the training data.

In order to extract the accuracy score, we use the following code on the test data:

```
#Accuracy score of the logistic regression model

logistic_regression.score(X_test, y_test)
```

This model has produced an accuracy of 58.9% on the test data. This means that the base logistic regression model only performs slightly better than an algorithm that randomly guesses the output.

Fine-tuning the hyperparameters

From the output of the logistic regression model implemented in the preceding section, it is clear that the model performs slightly better than random guessing. Such a model fails to provide value to us. In order to optimize the model, we are going to optimize the hyperparameters of the logistic regression model by using the GridSearchCV algorithm that we used in the previous chapter.

The hyperparameter that is used by the logistic regression model is known as the inverse regularization strength. This is because we are implementing a type of linear regression known as **l1** regression. This type of linear regression will explained in detail in Chapter 5, *Predicting Numeric Outcomes with Linear Regression*.

In order to optimize the inverse regularization strength, or **C** as it is called in short, we use the following code:

```
#Building the model with L1 penality

logistic_regression = linear_model.LogisticRegression(penalty='l1')

#Using GridSearchCV to search for the best parameter

grid = GridSearchCV(logistic_regression, {'C':[0.0001, 0.001, 0.01, 0.1,
10]})
grid.fit(X_train, y_train)

# Print out the best parameter

print("The most optimal inverse regularization strength is:",
grid.best_params_)
```

This produces an output as illustrated in the following screenshot:

```
The most optimal inverse regularization strength is: {'C': 10}
```

In the preceding code, we first initialize a logistic regression model with the penalty argument set to **l1**, indicating that we are using **l1** regression. We then initialize a grid with the possible values of inverse regularization strengths that go from 0.0001 to 10.

The number of values that you initialize in a grid object for the hyperparameter of a model is arbitrary. However, the more values, the longer it takes for GridSearchCV to give you the optimal value of the hyperparameter, therby making the process computationally expensive.

The grid object with the possible values of the inverse regularization strengths are then fit into the training data and the optimal value is printed out, which in this case is 10. We can now build a new logistic regression model with this newly obtained optimal hyperparameter value by using the following code:

```
#Initializing an logistic regression object

logistic_regression = linear_model.LogisticRegression(C = 10, penalty =
'l1')

#Fitting the model to the training and test sets

logistic_regression.fit(X_train, y_train)
```

Evaluating the model on the test data by using the following code, we obtain an accuracy score of 99.6%! That's quite the improvement.

```
#Accuracy score of the logistic regression model

logistic_regression.score(X_test, y_test)
```

One way to check whether `GridSearchCV` is giving us accurate results is to plot the accuracy scores along the y-axis for different values of the inverse regularization strengths along the x-axis. This can be done by using the following code:

```
train_errors = []
test_errors = []

C_list = [0.0001, 0.001, 0.01, 0.1, 10, 100, 1000]

# Evaluate the training and test classification errors for each value of C

for value in C_list:

 # Create LogisticRegression object and fit
 logistic_regression = linear_model.LogisticRegression(C= value, penalty =
'l1')
 logistic_regression.fit(X_train, y_train)

 # Evaluate error rates and append to lists
 train_errors.append(logistic_regression.score(X_train, y_train) )
 test_errors.append(logistic_regression.score(X_test, y_test))

# Plot results
plt.semilogx(C_list, train_errors, C_list, test_errors)
plt.legend(("train", "test"))
plt.ylabel('Accuracy Score')
```

```
plt.xlabel('C (Inverse regularization strength)')
plt.show()
```

This results in a plot as illustrated in the following diagram:

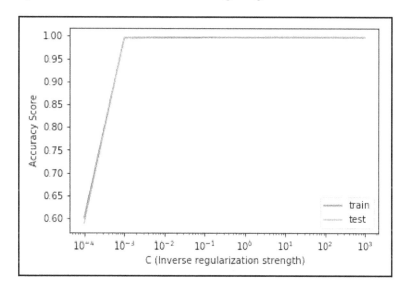

From the preceding plot, it is clear that an inverse regularization strength of 10 provides a high value of accuracy for both the training and testing sets. Such plots are also used to determine whether a particular value of the hyperparameter is overfitting the data by giving us a high accuracy score on the training set, but low accuracy scores on the test set. Conversely, they can also be used to check whether a model is undercutting the data by giving us low values of accuracy on the training set itself.

Scaling the data

Although the model has performed extremely well, scaling the data is still a useful step in building machine learning models with logistic regression, as it standardizes your data across the same range of values. In order to scale your data, we will use the same StandardScaler() function that we used in the previous chapter. This is done by using the following code:

```
from sklearn.preprocessing import StandardScaler
from sklearn.pipeline import Pipeline

#Setting up the scaling pipeline
```

```
pipeline_order = [('scaler', StandardScaler()), ('logistic_reg',
linear_model.LogisticRegression(C = 10, penalty = 'l1'))]

pipeline = Pipeline(pipeline_order)

#Fitting the classfier to the scaled dataset

logistic_regression_scaled = pipeline.fit(X_train, y_train)

#Extracting the score

logistic_regression_scaled.score(X_test, y_test)
```

The preceding code resulted in the improvement in the accuracy score of the model by 0.1%, which is good considering how the model had a very high accuracy score in the first place. The code is similar to the pipeline for scaling we built in the previous chapter for the k-NN algorithm, and there are no changes except for the fact that we have used a logistic regression model instead of the k-NN model.

Interpreting the logistic regression model

One of the key benefits of the logistic regression algorithm is that it is highly interpretable. This means that the outcome of the model can be interpreted as a function of the input variables. This allows us to understand how each variable contributes to the eventual outcome of the model.

In the first section, we understood that the logistic regression model consists of coefficients for each variable and an intercept that can be used to explain how the model works. In order to extract the coefficients for each variable in the model, we use the following code:

```
#Printing out the coefficients of each variable

print(logistic_regression.coef_)
```

This results in an output as illustrated by the following screenshot:

```
[[  4.80188666e-05   1.59768979e-01   2.51418163e-01  -4.70355274e-06
    2.36326041e-05  -3.43658187e-05  -1.55507920e-06  -8.30036365e-08
   -1.13670693e+01  -9.12306047e+00  -1.67613709e+01  -1.17033896e+01
   -9.11703172e+00]]
```

The coefficients are in the order in which the variables were in the dataset that was input into the model. In order to extract the intercept from the model, we use the following code:

```
#Printing out the intercept of the model

print(logistic_regression.intercept_)
```

This results in an output as shown in the following screenshot:

```
[ 2.68799332]
```

Now that we have the coefficients for each variable along with the intercept, we can construct an equation in the following form:

$$ModelOutput = \sum (Variables \times Coefficients) + Intercept$$

Summary

In this chapter, you have learned how the logistic regression model works on a mathematical level. Although simplistic, the model proves to be formidable in terms of interpretability, which is highly beneficial in the financial industry.

You have also learned how to build and evaluate logistic regression algorithms using scikit-learn, and looked at hyperparameter optimization using the GridSearchCV algorithm. Additionally, you have learned to verify whether the results provided to you by the GridSearchCV algorithm are accurate by plotting the accuracy scores for different values of the hyperparameter.

Finally, you have scaled your data in order make it standardized and learned how to interpret your model on a mathematical level.

In the next chapter, you will learn how to implement tree-based algorithms, such as decision trees, random forests, and gradient-boosted trees, using scikit-learn.

4
Predicting Categories with Naive Bayes and SVMs

In this chapter, you will learn about two popular classification machine learning algorithms: the Naive Bayes algorithm and the linear support vector machine. The Naive Bayes algorithm is a probabilistic model that predicts classes and categories, while the linear support vector machine uses a linear decision boundary to predict classes and categories.

In this chapter, you will learn about the following topics:

- The theoretical concept behind the Naive Bayes algorithm, explained in mathematical terms
- Implementing the Naive Bayes algorithm by using scikit-learn
- How the linear support vector machine algorithm works under the hood
- Graphically optimizing the hyperparameters of the linear support vector machines

Technical requirements

You will be required to have Python 3.6 or greater, Pandas ≥ 0.23.4, Scikit-learn ≥ 0.20.0, and Matplotlib ≥ 3.0.0 installed on your system.

The code files of this chapter can be found on GitHub:
`https://github.com/PacktPublishing/Machine-Learning-with-scikit-learn-Quick-Start-Guide/blob/master/Chapter_04.ipynb`

Check out the following video to see the code in action:

`http://bit.ly/2COBMUj`

The Naive Bayes algorithm

The Naive Bayes algorithm makes use of the Bayes theorem, in order to classify classes and categories. The word **naive** was given to the algorithm because the algorithm assumes that all attributes are independent of one another. This is not actually possible, as every attribute/feature in a dataset is related to another attribute, in one way or another.

Despite being naive, the algorithm does well in actual practice. The formula for the Bayes theorem is as follows:

$$p(h|\mathcal{D}) = \frac{p(\mathcal{D}|h)p(h)}{p(\mathcal{D})}$$

Bayes theorem formula

We can split the preceding algorithm into the following components:

- **p(h|D)**: This is the probability of a hypothesis taking place, provided that we have a dataset. An example of this would be the probability of a fraudulent transaction taking place, provided that we had a dataset that consisted of fraudulent and non-fraudulent transactions.
- **p(D|h)**: This is the probability of having the data, given a hypothesis. An example of this would be the probability of having a dataset that contained fraudulent transactions.
- **p(h)**: This is the probability of a hypothesis taking place, in general. An example of this would be a statement that the average probability of fraudulent transactions taking place in the mobile industry is 2%.
- **p(D)**: This is the probability of having the data before knowing any hypothesis. An example of this would be the probability that a dataset of mobile transactions could be found without knowing what we wanted to do with it (for example, predict fraudulent mobile transactions).

In the preceding formula, the *p(D)* can be rewritten in terms of *p(h)* and *p(D|h)*, as follows:

$$p(h|\mathcal{D}) = \frac{p(\mathcal{D}|h)p(h)}{p(\mathcal{D}|h)p(h) + p(\mathcal{D}|\neg h)(1 - p(h))}$$

Let's take a look at how we can implement this with the method of predicting classes, in the case of the mobile transaction example:

p(D|h)	p(h)	p(D|-h)	(1 - p(h))
0.8	0.08	0.02	0.92

Substituting the values in the preceding table into the Bayes theorem formula produces a result of 0.77. This means that the classifier predicts that there is a 77% probability that a transaction will be predicted as fraudulent, using the data that was given previously.

Implementing the Naive Bayes algorithm in scikit-learn

Now that you have learned how the Naive Bayes algorithm generates predictions, we will implement the same classifier using scikit-learn, in order to predict whether a particular transaction is fraudulent.

The first step is to import the data, create the feature and target arrays, and split the data into training and test sets.

We can do this by using the following code:

```
import pandas as pd
from sklearn.model_selection import train_test_split

df = pd.read_csv('fraud_prediction.csv')

df = df.drop(['Unnamed: 0'], axis = 1)

#Creating the features

features = df.drop('isFraud', axis = 1).values
target = df['isFraud'].values

X_train, X_test, y_train, y_test = train_test_split(features, target,
test_size = 0.3, random_state = 42, stratify = target)
```

The next step is to build the Naive Bayes classifier. We can do this by using the following code:

```
from sklearn.naive_bayes import GaussianNB

#Initializing an NB classifier

nb_classifier = GaussianNB()

#Fitting the classifier into the training data

nb_classifier.fit(X_train, y_train)

#Extracting the accuracy score from the NB classifier

nb_classifier.score(X_test, y_test)
```

In the preceding code, the following applies:

1. First, we import the `GaussianNB` module from scikit-learn
2. Next, we initialize a Naive Bayes classifier and store it in the variable `nb_classifier`
3. Then, we fit the classifier to the training data and evaluate its accuracy on the test data

The Naive Bayes classifier has only one hyperparameter, which is the prior probability of the hypothesis, *p(h)*. However, keep the following in mind:

- The prior probability will not be available to us in most problems
- Even if it is, the value is usually fixed as a statistical fact, and therefore, hyperparameter optimization is not performed

Support vector machines

In this section, you will learn about **support vector machines (SVMs)**, or, to be more specific, **linear support vector machines**. In order to understand support vector machines, you will need to know what support vectors are. They are illustrated for you in the following diagram:

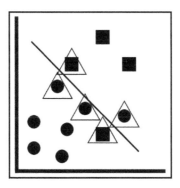

The concept of support vectors

In the preceding diagram, the following applies:

- The linear support vector machine is a form of linear classifier. A linear decision tree boundary is constructed, and the observations on one side of the boundary (the circles) belong to one class, while the observations on the other side of the boundary (the squares) belong to another class.
- The support vectors are the observations that have a triangle on them.
- These are the observations that are either very close to the linear decision boundary or have been incorrectly classified.
- We can define which observations we want to make support vectors by defining how close to the decision boundary they should be.
- This is controlled by the hyperparameter known as the **inverse regularization strength.**

In order to understand how the linear support vector machines work, consider the following diagram:

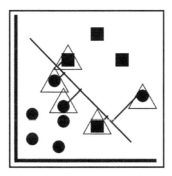

Concept of max-margins

In the preceding diagram, the following applies:

- The line between the support vectors and the linear decision boundary is known as the **margin**
- The goal of the support vector machines is to maximize this margin, so that a new data point will be correctly classified
- A low value of inverse regularization strength ensures that this margin is as big as possible

Implementing the linear support vector machine algorithm in scikit-learn

In this section, you will learn how to implement the linear support vector machines in scikit-learn. The first step is to import the data and split it into training and testing sets. We can do this by using the following code:

```
import pandas as pd
from sklearn.model_selection import train_test_split

df = pd.read_csv('fraud_prediction.csv')

df = df.drop(['Unnamed: 0'], axis = 1)

#Creating the features

features = df.drop('isFraud', axis = 1).values
target = df['isFraud'].values

X_train, X_test, y_train, y_test = train_test_split(features, target,
test_size = 0.3, random_state = 42, stratify = target)
```

The next step is to build the linear support vector machine classifier. We can do this by using the following code:

```
from sklearn.svm import LinearSVC

#Initializing a SVM model

svm = LinearSVC(random_state = 50)

#Fitting the model to the training data

svm.fit(X_train, y_train)
```

```
#Extracting the accuracy score from the training data

svm.score(X_test, y_test)
```

In the preceding code, the following applies:

1. First, we import the `LinearSVC` module from scikit-learn
2. Next, we initialize a linear support vector machine object with a random state of 50, so that the model produces the same result every time
3. Finally, we fit the model to the training data and evaluate its accuracy on the test data

Now that we have built the model, we can find and optimize the most ideal value for the hyperparameters.

Hyperparameter optimization for the linear SVMs

In this section, you will learn how to optimize the hyperparameters for the linear support vector machines. In particular, there is one hyperparameter of interest: the **inverse regularization strength**.

We will explore how to optimize this hyperparameter, both graphically and algorithmically.

Graphical hyperparameter optimization

In order to optimize the inverse regularization strength, we will plot the accuracy scores for the training and testing sets, using the following code:

```
import matplotlib.pyplot as plt
from sklearn.svm import LinearSVC

training_scores = []
testing_scores = []

param_list = [0.0001, 0.001, 0.01, 0.1, 10, 100, 1000]

# Evaluate the training and test classification errors for each value of
the parameter

for param in param_list:
    # Create SVM object and fit
    svm = LinearSVC(C = param, random_state = 42)
```

```
        svm.fit(X_train, y_train)
        # Evaluate the accuracy scores and append to lists
        training_scores.append(svm.score(X_train, y_train) )
        testing_scores.append(svm.score(X_test, y_test) )
    # Plot results

plt.semilogx(param_list, training_scores, param_list, testing_scores)
plt.legend(("train", "test"))
plt.ylabel('Accuracy scores')
plt.xlabel('C (Inverse regularization strength)')
plt.show()
```

In the preceding code, the following applies:

1. First, we initialize two empty lists, in order to store the accuracy scores for both the training and testing datasets
2. The next step is to create a list of values of the hyperparameter, which, in this case, is the inverse regularization strength
3. We then loop over each value in the hyperparameter list and build a linear support vector machine classifier with each inverse regularization strength value
4. The accuracy scores for the training and testing datasets are then appended to the empty lists
5. Using `matplotlib`, we then create a plot between the inverse regularization strength (along the *x* axis) and the accuracy scores for both the training and test sets (along the *y* axis)

This will produce a plot as shown in the following diagram:

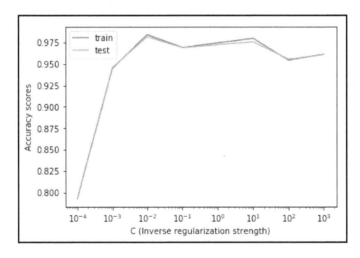

Graphical hyperparameter optimization

In the preceding diagram, the following applies:

- We can observe that the accuracy score is highest for the training and testing sets for an inverse regularization strength of 10^{-2}
- It is important to pick a value that has a high value of accuracy for both the training and testing sets, and not just either one of the datasets
- This will help you to prevent both overfitting and underfitting

Hyperparameter optimization using GridSearchCV

In this section, you will learn how to optimize the inverse regularization strength using the GridSearchCV algorithm. We can do this using the following code:

```
from sklearn.model_selection import GridSearchCV

#Building the model

svm = LinearSVC(random_state = 50)

#Using GridSearchCV to search for the best parameter

grid = GridSearchCV(svm, {'C':[0.00001, 0.0001, 0.001, 0.01, 0.1, 10]})
grid.fit(X_train, y_train)

# Print out the best parameter

print("The best value of the inverse regularization strength is:",
grid.best_params_)
```

In the preceding code, the following applies:

1. First, we import the GridSearchCV module from scikit-learn
2. The next step is to initialize a linear support vector machine model with a random state of 50, in order to ensure that we obtain the same results every time we build the model
3. We then initialize a grid of possible hyperparameter values for the inverse regularization strength
4. Finally, we fit the grid of hyperparameter values to the training set, so that we can build multiple linear SVM models with the different values of the inverse regularization strength
5. The GridSearchCV algorithm then evaluates the model that produces the fewest generalization errors and returns the optimal value of the hyperparameter

It's a good practice to compare and contrast the results of the graphical method of hyperparameter optimization with that of GridSearchCV, in order to validate your results.

Scaling the data for performance improvement

In this section, you will learn about how scaling and standardizing the data can lead to an improvement in the overall performance of the linear support vector machines. The concept of scaling remains the same as in the case of the previous chapters, and it will not be discussed here. In order to scale the data, we use the following code:

```
from sklearn.preprocessing import StandardScaler
from sklearn.pipeline import Pipeline

#Setting up the scaling pipeline

order = [('scaler', StandardScaler()), ('SVM', LinearSVC(C = 0.1,
random_state = 50))]

pipeline = Pipeline(order)

#Fitting the classfier to the scaled dataset

svm_scaled = pipeline.fit(X_train, y_train)

#Extracting the score

svm_scaled.score(X_test, y_test)
```

In the preceding code, the following applies:

1. First, we import the StandardScaler the Pipeline modules from scikit-learn, in order to build a scaling pipeline
2. We then set up the order of the pipeline, which specifies that we use the StandardScaler() function first, in order to scale the data and build the linear support vector machine on that scaled data
3. The Pipeline() function is applied to the order of the pipeline which sets up the pipeline
4. We then fit this pipeline to the training data and extract the scaled accuracy scores from the test data

Summary

This chapter introduced you to two fundamental supervised machine learning algorithms: the Naive Bayes algorithm and linear support vector machines. More specifically, you learned about the following topics:

- How the Bayes theorem is used to produce a probability, to indicate whether a data point belongs to a particular class or category
- Implementing the Naive Bayes classifier in scikit-learn
- How the linear support vector machines work under the hood
- Implementing the linear support vector machines in scikit-learn
- Optimizing the inverse regularization strength, both graphically and by using the `GridSearchCV` algorithm
- How to scale your data for a potential improvement in performance

In the next chapter, you will learn about the other type of supervised machine learning algorithm, which is used to predict numeric values, rather than classes and categories: linear regression!

5
Predicting Numeric Outcomes with Linear Regression

graph_from_dot_data() function on the Linear regression is used to predict a continuous numeric value from a set of input features. This machine learning algorithm is fundamental to statisticians when it comes to predicting numeric outcomes. Although advanced algorithms such as neural networks and deep learning have taken the place of linear regression in modern times, the algorithm is still key when it comes to providing you with the foundations for neural networks and deep learning.

The key benefit of building machine learning models with the linear regression algorithm, as opposed to neural networks and deep learning, is that it is highly interpretable. Interpretability helps you, as the machine learning practitioner, to understand how the different input variables behave when it comes to predicting output.

The linear regression algorithm is applied in the financial industry (in order to predict stock prices) and in the real estate industry (in order to predict housing prices). In fact, the linear regression algorithm can be applied in any field where there is a need to predict a numeric value, given a set of input features.

In this chapter, you will learn about the following topics:

- The inner mechanics of the linear regression algorithm
- Building and evaluating your first linear regression algorithm, using scikit-learn
- Scaling your data for a potential performance improvement
- Optimizing your linear regression model

Technical requirements

You will be required to have Python 3.6 or greater, Pandas ≥ 0.23.4, Scikit-learn ≥ 0.20.0, and Matplotlib ≥ 3.0.0 installed on your system.

The code files of this chapter can be found on GitHub:
`https://github.com/PacktPublishing/Machine-Learning-with-scikit-learn-Quick-Start-Guide/blob/master/Chapter_05.ipynb`

Check out the following video to see the code in action:

`http://bit.ly/2Ay95cJ`

The inner mechanics of the linear regression algorithm

In its most fundamental form, the expression for the linear regression algorithm can be written as follows:

$$NumericOutput = \sum (InputFeatures \times Parameter1) + Parameter2$$

In the preceding equation, the output of the model is a numeric outcome. In order to obtain this numeric outcome, we require that each input feature be multiplied with a parameter called *Parameter1*, and we add the second parameter, *Parameter2*, to this result.

So, in other words, our task is to find the values of the two parameters that can predict the value of the numeric outcome as accurately as possible. In visual terms, consider the following diagram:

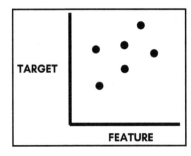

Two-dimensional plot between the target and input feature

The preceding diagram shows a two-dimensional plot between the target that we want to predict on the y axis (numeric output) and the input feature, which is along the x axis. The goal of linear regression is to find the optimal values of the two parameters mentioned in the preceding equation, in order to fit a line through the given set of points.

This line is known as the **line of best fit**. A line of best fit is one that fits the given sets of points very well, so that it can make accurate predictions for us. Therefore, in order to find the optimal values of the parameters that will result in the line of best fit, we need to define a function that can do it for us.

This function is known as the **loss function**. The goal of the loss function, as the name suggests, is to minimize the loss/errors as much as possible, so that we can obtain a line of best fit. In order to understand how this works, consider the following diagram:

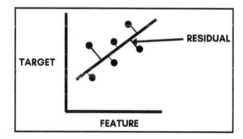

Line of best fit

In the preceding diagram, the line is fit through the set of data points, and the features can be defined as follows:

- The distance between each point in the plot and the line is known as the **residual**.
- The loss/error function is the sum of the squares of these residuals.
- The goal of the linear regression algorithm is to minimize this value. The sum of the squares of the residuals is known as **ordinary least squares (OLS)**.

Implementing linear regression in scikit-learn

In this section, you will implement your first linear regression algorithm in scikit-learn. To make this easy to follow, the section will be divided into three subsections, in which you will learn about the following topics:

- Implementing and visualizing a simple linear regression model in two dimensions
- Implementing linear regression to predict the mobile transaction amount
- Scaling your data for a potential increase in performance

Linear regression in two dimensions

In this subsection, you will learn how to implement your first linear regression algorithm, in order to predict the amount of a mobile transaction by using one input feature: the old balance amount of the account holder. We will be using the same fraudulent mobile transaction dataset that we used in *Chapter 2, Predicting Categories with K-Nearest Neighbors,* of this book.

The first step is to read in the dataset and define the feature and target variable. This can be done by using the following code:

```
import pandas as pd

#Reading in the dataset

df = pd.read_csv('fraud_prediction.csv')

#Define the feature and target arrays

feature = df['oldbalanceOrg'].values
target = df['amount'].values
```

Next, we will create a simple scatter plot between the amount of the mobile transaction on the *y* axis (which is the outcome of the linear regression model) and the old balance of the account holder along the *x* axis (which is the input feature). This can be done by using the following code:

```
import matplotlib.pyplot as plt

#Creating a scatter plot

plt.scatter(feature, target)
plt.xlabel('Old Balance of Account Holder')
plt.ylabel('Amount of Transaction')
plt.title('Amount Vs. Old Balance')
plt.show()
```

In the preceding code, we use the `plt.scatter()` function to create a scatter plot between the feature on the *x* axis and the target on the *y* axis. This results in the scatter plot illustrated in the following diagram:

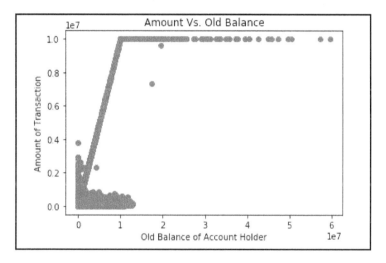

Two-dimensional space of the linear regression model

Now, we will fit a linear regression model into the two-dimensional space illustrated in the preceding diagram. Note that, in the preceding diagram, the data is not entirely linear. In order to do this, we use the following code:

```
#Initializing a linear regression model

linear_reg = linear_model.LinearRegression()

#Reshaping the array since we only have a single feature

feature = feature.reshape(-1, 1)
target = target.reshape(-1, 1)

#Fitting the model on the data
```

```
linear_reg.fit(feature, target)

#Define the limits of the x axis

x_lim = np.linspace(min(feature), max(feature)).reshape(-1, 1)

#Creating the scatter plot

plt.scatter(feature, target)
plt.xlabel('Old Balance of Account Holder')
plt.ylabel('Amount of Transaction')
plt.title('Amount Vs. Old Balance')

#Creating the prediction line

plt.plot(x_lim, linear_reg.predict(x_lim), color = 'red')

#Show the plot

plt.show()
```

This results in a line of best fit, as illustrated in the following diagram:

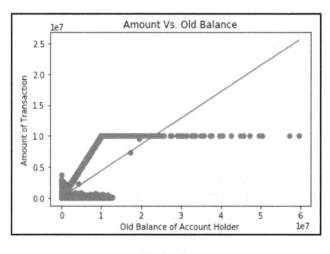

Line of best fit

In the preceding code, first, we initialize a linear regression model and fit the training data into that model. Since we only have a single feature, we need to reshape the feature and target for scikit-learn. Next, we define the upper and lower limits of the x axis, which contains our feature variable.

Finally, we create a scatter plot between the feature and the target variable and include the line of best fit with the color red, as indicated in the preceding diagram.

Using linear regression to predict mobile transaction amount

Now that we have visualized how a simple linear regression model works in two dimensions, we can use the linear regression algorithm to predict the total amount of a mobile transaction, using all of the other features in our mobile transaction dataset.

The first step is to import our fraud prediction dataset into our workspace and divide it into training and test sets. This can be done by using the following code:

```
import pandas as pd
from sklearn.model_selection import train_test_split

# Reading in the dataset

df = pd.read_csv('fraud_prediction.csv')

#Creating the features

features = df.drop('isFraud', axis = 1).values
target = df['isFraud'].values

X_train, X_test, y_train, y_test = train_test_split(features, target,
test_size = 0.3, random_state = 42, stratify = target)
```

We can now fit the linear regression model and evaluate the initial accuracy score of the model by using the following code:

```
from sklearn import linear_model

#Initializing a linear regression model

linear_reg = linear_model.LinearRegression()

#Fitting the model on the data

linear_reg.fit(X_train, y_train)

#Accuracy of the model

linear_reg.score(X_test, y_test)
```

In the preceding code, first, we initialize a linear regression model, which we can then fit into the training data by using the `.fit()` function. Then, we evaluate the accuracy score on the test data by using the `.score()` function. This results in an accuracy score of 98%, which is fantastic!

Scaling your data

Scaling your data and providing a level of standardization is a vital step in any linear regression pipeline, as it could offer a way to enhance the performance of your model. In order to scale the data, we use the following code:

```
from sklearn.preprocessing import StandardScaler
from sklearn.pipeline import Pipeline

#Setting up the scaling pipeline

pipeline_order = [('scaler', StandardScaler()), ('linear_reg',
linear_model.LinearRegression())]

pipeline = Pipeline(pipeline_order)

#Fitting the classfier to the scaled dataset

linear_reg_scaled = pipeline.fit(X_train, y_train)

#Extracting the score

linear_reg_scaled.score(X_test, y_test)
```

We use the same scaling pipeline that we used in all of the previous chapters. In the preceding code, we replace the model name with the linear regression model and evaluate the scaled accuracy scores on the test data.

In this case, scaling the data did not lead to any improvements in the accuracy score, but it is vital to implement scaling into your linear regression pipeline, as it does lead to an improvement in the accuracy scores in most cases.

Model optimization

The fundamental objective of the linear regression algorithm is to minimize the loss/cost function. In order to do this, the algorithm tries to optimize the values of the coefficients of each feature (*Parameter1*), such that the loss function is minimized.

Sometimes, this leads to overfitting, as the coefficients of each variable are optimized for the data that the variable is trained on. This means that your linear regression model will not generalize beyond your current training data very well.

The process by which we penalize hyper-optimized coefficients in order to prevent this type of overfitting is called **regularization**.

There are two broad types of regularization methods, as follows:

- Ridge regression
- Lasso regression

In the following subsections, the two types of regularization techniques will be discussed in detail, and you will learn about how you can implement them into your model.

Ridge regression

The equation for ridge regression is as follows:

$$RidgeLossFunction = OLSFunction + (Alpha \times \sum Parameter1^2)$$

In the preceding equation, the ridge loss function is equal to the ordinary least squares loss function, plus the product of the square of *Parameter1* of each feature and `alpha`.

`alpha` is a parameter that we can optimize in order to control the amount by which the ridge loss function penalizes the coefficients, in order to prevent overfitting. Obviously, if `alpha` is equal to `0`, the ridge loss function is equal to the ordinary least squares loss function, thereby making no difference to the initial overfit model.

Therefore, optimizing this value of `alpha` provides the optimal model that can generalize beyond the data that it has trained on.

In order to implement ridge regression into the fraud prediction dataset, we use the following code:

```
from sklearn.linear_model import Ridge
import pandas as pd
import numpy as np
from sklearn.model_selection import train_test_split
from sklearn.linear_model import Ridge

# Reading in the dataset
```

```
df = pd.read_csv('fraud_prediction.csv')

#Creating the features

features = df.drop('isFraud', axis = 1).values
target = df['isFraud'].values

X_train, X_test, y_train, y_test = train_test_split(features, target,
test_size = 0.3, random_state = 42, stratify = target)

#Initialize a ridge regression model

ridge_reg = Ridge(alpha = 0, normalize = True)

#Fit the model to the training data

ridge_reg.fit(X_train, y_train)

#Extract the score from the test data

ridge_reg.score(X_test, y_test)
```

In the preceding code, first, we read in the dataset and divide it into training and test sets (as usual). Next, we initialize a ridge regression model by using the `Ridge()` function, with the parameters of `alpha` set to 0 and `normalize` set to `True`, in order to standardize the data.

Next, the ridge model is fit into the training data, and the accuracy score is extracted from the test data. The accuracy of this model is exactly the same as the accuracy of the model that we built without the ridge regression as the parameter that controls how the model is optimized; `alpha` is set to 0.

In order to obtain the optimal value of `alpha` with the `GridSearchCV` algorithm, we use the following code:

```
from sklearn.model_selection import GridSearchCV

#Building the model

ridge_regression = Ridge()

#Using GridSearchCV to search for the best parameter

grid = GridSearchCV(ridge_regression, {'alpha':[0.0001, 0.001, 0.01, 0.1,
10]})
grid.fit(X_train, y_train)
```

```
# Print out the best parameter

print("The most optimal value of alpha is:", grid.best_params_)

#Initializing an ridge regression object

ridge_regression = Ridge(alpha = 0.01)

#Fitting the model to the training and test sets

ridge_regression.fit(X_train, y_train)

#Accuracy score of the ridge regression model

ridge_regression.score(X_test, y_test)
```

In the preceding code, the following applies:

1. First, we initialize a ridge regression model, and then, we use the `GridSearchCV` algorithm to search for the optimal value of `alpha`, from a range of values.
2. After we obtain this optimal value of `alpha`, we build a new ridge regression model with this optimal value in the training data, and we evaluate the accuracy score on the test data.

Since our initial model was already well optimized, the accuracy score did not increase by an observable amount. However, on datasets with larger dimensions/features, ridge regression holds immense value for providing you with a model that generalizes well, without overfitting.

In order to verify the results that the `GridSearchCV` algorithm has provided us with, we will construct a plot between the accuracy scores on the *y* axis and the different values of `alpha` along the *x* axis, for both the training and test data. In order to do this, we use the following code:

```
import matplotlib.pyplot as plt

train_errors = []
test_errors = []

alpha_list = [0.0001, 0.001, 0.01, 0.1, 10]

# Evaluate the training and test classification errors for each value of
alpha

for value in alpha_list:
    # Create Ridge object and fit
```

```
        ridge_regression = Ridge(alpha= value)
        ridge_regression.fit(X_train, y_train)
        # Evaluate error rates and append to lists
        train_errors.append(ridge_regression.score(X_train, y_train) )
        test_errors.append(ridge_regression.score(X_test, y_test))
    # Plot results
    plt.semilogx(alpha_list, train_errors, alpha_list, test_errors)
    plt.legend(("train", "test"))
    plt.ylabel('Accuracy Score')
    plt.xlabel('Alpha')
    plt.show()
```

This results in the following output:

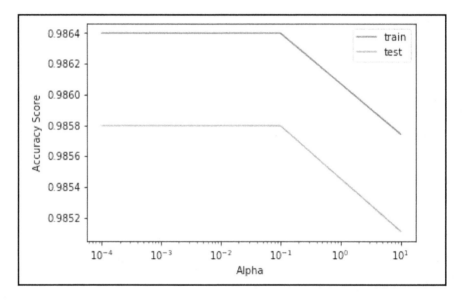

Accuracy versus alpha

In the preceding plot, it is clear that a value of 0.01 or lower provides the highest value of accuracy for both the training and test data, and therefore, the results from the `GridSearchCV` algorithm make logical sense.

In the preceding code, first, we initialize two empty lists, to store the accuracy scores for both the training and test data. We then evaluate the accuracy scores for both the training and test sets for different values of `alpha`, and we create the preceding plot.

Lasso regression

The equation for lasso regression is as follows:

$$LassoLossFunction = OLSFunction + (Alpha \times \sum |Parameter1|)$$

In the preceding equation, the lasso loss function is equal to the ordinary least squares loss function plus the product of the absolute value of the coefficients of each feature and `alpha`.

`alpha` is a parameter that we can optimize to control the amount by which the lasso loss function penalizes the coefficients, in order to prevent overfitting. Once again, if `alpha` is equal to 0, the lasso loss function is equal to the ordinary least squares loss function, thereby making no difference to the initial overfit model.

Therefore, optimizing this value of `alpha` provides the optimal model that generalizes well beyond the data that it has trained on.

In order to implement lasso regression into the fraud prediction dataset, we use the following code:

```
import pandas as pd
import numpy as np
from sklearn.model_selection import train_test_split
from sklearn.linear_model import Lasso
import warnings

# Reading in the dataset

df = pd.read_csv('fraud_prediction.csv')

#Creating the features

features = df.drop('isFraud', axis = 1).values
target = df['isFraud'].values

X_train, X_test, y_train, y_test = train_test_split(features, target,
test_size = 0.3, random_state = 42, stratify = target)

#Initialize a lasso regression model

lasso_reg = Lasso(alpha = 0, normalize = True)

#Fit the model to the training data
```

```
lasso_reg.fit(X_train, y_train)

warnings.filterwarnings('ignore')

#Extract the score from the test data

lasso_reg.score(X_test, y_test)
```

The preceding code is very similar to the code that we used to build the ridge regression model; the only difference is the `Lasso()` function which we use to initialize a lasso regression model. Additionally, the `warnings` package is used, in order to suppress the warning that is generated as we set the value of `alpha` to 0.

In order to optimize the value of `alpha`, we use the `GridSearchCV` algorithm. This is done by using the following code:

```
from sklearn.model_selection import GridSearchCV

#Building the model

lasso_regression = Lasso()

#Using GridSearchCV to search for the best parameter

grid = GridSearchCV(lasso_regression, {'alpha':[0.0001, 0.001, 0.01, 0.1,
10]})
grid.fit(X_train, y_train)

# Print out the best parameter

print("The most optimal value of alpha is:", grid.best_params_)

#Initializing an lasso regression object

lasso_regression = Lasso(alpha = 0.0001)

#Fitting the model to the training and test sets

lasso_regression.fit(X_train, y_train)

#Accuracy score of the lasso regression model

lasso_regression.score(X_test, y_test)
```

The preceding code is similar to the `alpha` optimization that we implemented for the ridge regression. Here, we use the lasso regression model instead of the ridge regression model.

In order to verify the results of the `GridSearchCV` algorithm, we construct a plot between the accuracy scores and the value of `alpha` for the training and test sets. This is shown in the following code:

```
train_errors = []
test_errors = []

alpha_list = [0.0001, 0.001, 0.01, 0.1, 10]

# Evaluate the training and test classification errors for each value of
alpha

for value in alpha_list:
    # Create Lasso object and fit
    lasso_regression = Lasso(alpha= value)
    lasso_regression.fit(X_train, y_train)
    # Evaluate error rates and append to lists
    train_errors.append(ridge_regression.score(X_train, y_train) )
    test_errors.append(ridge_regression.score(X_test, y_test))
# Plot results
plt.semilogx(alpha_list, train_errors, alpha_list, test_errors)
plt.legend(("train", "test"))
plt.ylabel('Accuracy Score')
plt.xlabel('Alpha')
plt.show()
```

This results in the following output:

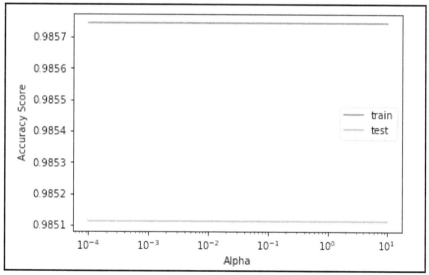

Accuracy versus alpha

All of the values of `alpha` provide the same values of accuracy scores, and we can thus pick the value given to us by the `GridSearchCV` algorithm.

Summary

In this chapter, you learned about how the linear regression algorithm works internally, through key concepts such as residuals and ordinary least squares. You also learned how to visualize a simple linear regression model in two dimensions.

We also covered implementing the linear regression model to predict the amount of a mobile transaction, along with scaling your data in an effective pipeline, to bring potential improvements to your performance.

Finally, you learned how to optimize your model by using the concept of regularization, in the form of ridge and lasso regression.

6

Classification and Regression with Trees

Tree based algorithms are very popular for two reasons: they are interpretable, and they make sound predictions that have won many machine learning competitions on online platforms, such as Kaggle. Furthermore, they have many use cases outside of machine learning for solving problems, both simple and complex.

Building a tree is an approach to decision-making used in almost all industries. Trees can be used to solve both classification- and regression-based problems, and have several use cases that make them the go-to solution!

This chapter is broadly divided into the following two sections:

- Classification trees
- Regression trees

Each section will cover the fundamental theory of different types of tree based algorithms, along with their implementation in scikit-learn. By the end of this chapter, you will have learned how to aggregate several algorithms into an **ensemble** and have them vote on what the best prediction is.

Technical requirements

You will be required to have Python 3.6 or greater, Pandas ≥ 0.23.4, Scikit-learn ≥ 0.20.0, and Matplotlib ≥ 3.0.0 installed on your system.

The code files of this chapter can be found on GitHub:
https://github.com/PacktPublishing/Machine-Learning-with-scikit-learn-Quick-Start-Guide/blob/master/Chapter_06.ipynb.

Check out the following video to see the code in action:

`http://bit.ly/2SrPP7R`

Classification trees

Classification trees are used to predict a category or class. This is similar to the classification algorithms that you have learned about previously in this book, such as the k-nearest neighbors algorithm or logistic regression.

Broadly speaking, there are three tree based algorithms that are used to solve classification problems:

- The decision tree classifier
- The random forest classifier
- The AdaBoost classifier

In this section, you will learn how each of these tree based algorithms works, in order to classify a row of data as a particular class or category.

The decision tree classifier

The decision tree is the simplest tree based algorithm, and serves as the foundation for the other two algorithms. Let's consider the following simple decision tree:

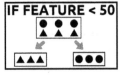

A simple decision tree

A decision tree, in simple terms, is a set of rules that help us classify observations into distinct groups. In the previous diagram, the rule could be written as the following:

```
If (value of feature is less than 50); then (put the triangles in the left-
hand box and put the circles in the right-hand box).
```

The preceding decision tree perfectly divides the observations into two distinct groups. This is a characteristic of the ideal decision tree. The first box on the top is called the **root** of the tree, and is the most important feature of the tree when it comes to deciding how to group the observations.

The boxes under the root node are known as the **children**. In the preceding tree, the **children** are also the **leaf** nodes. The **leaf** is the last set of boxes, usually in the bottommost part of the tree. As you might have guessed, the decision tree represents a regular tree, but inverted, or upside down.

Picking the best feature

How does the decision tree decide which feature is the best? The best feature is one that offers the best possible split, and divides the tree into two or more distinct groups, depending on the number of classes or categories that we have in the data. Let's have a look at the following diagram:

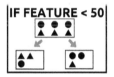

A decision tree showing a good split

In the preceding diagram, the following happens:

1. The tree splits the data from the root node into two distinct groups.
2. In the left-hand group, we see that there are two triangles and one circle.
3. In the right-hand group, we see that there are two circles and one triangle.
4. Since the tree got the majority of each class into one group, we can say that the tree has done a good job when it comes to splitting the data into distinct groups.

Let's take a look at another example—this time, one in which the split is bad. Consider the following diagram:

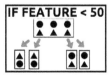

A decision tree with a bad split

In the preceding diagram, the following happens:

1. The tree splits the data in the root node into four distinct groups. This is bad in itself, as it is clear that there are only two categories (circle and triangle).
2. Furthermore, each group has one triangle and one circle.
3. There is no majority class or category in any one of the four groups. Each group has 50% of one category; therefore, the tree cannot come to a conclusive decision, unless it relies on more features, which then increases the complexity of the tree.

The Gini coefficient

The metric that the decision tree uses to decide if the root node is called the *Gini coefficient*. The higher the value of this coefficient, the better the job that this particular feature does at splitting the data into distinct groups. In order to learn how to compute the Gini coefficient for a feature, let's consider the following diagram:

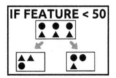

Computing the Gini coefficient

In the preceding diagram, the following happens:

1. The feature splits the data into two groups.
2. In the left-hand group, we have two triangles and one circle.
3. Therefore, the Gini for the left-hand group is (2 triangles/3 total data points)^2+ (1 circle/3 total data points)^2.
4. To calculate this, do the following: $2/3^2 + 1/3^2 = 0.55$.
5. A value of 0.55 for the Gini coefficient indicates that the root of this tree splits the data in such a way that each group has a majority category.
6. A perfect root feature would have a Gini coefficient of 1. This means that each group has only one class/category.
7. A bad root feature would have a Gini coefficient of 0.5, which indicates that there is no distinct class/category in a group.

In reality, the decision tree is built in a recursive manner, with the tree picking a random attribute for the root and then computing the Gini coefficient for that attribute. It does this until it finds the attribute that best splits the data in a node into groups that have distinct classes and categories.

Implementing the decision tree classifier in scikit-learn

In this section, you will learn how to implement the decision tree classifier in scikit-learn. We will work with the same fraud detection dataset. The first step is to load the dataset into the Jupyter Notebook. We can do this by using the following code:

```
import pandas as pd

df = pd.read_csv('fraud_prediction.csv')
```

The next step is to split the data into training and test sets. We can do this using the following code:

```
#Creating the features

features = df.drop('isFraud', axis = 1).values
target = df['isFraud'].values

X_train, X_test, y_train, y_test = train_test_split(features, target,
test_size = 0.3, random_state = 42, stratify = target)
```

We can now build the initial decision tree classifier on the training data, and test its accuracy on the test data, by using the following code:

```
from sklearn.tree import DecisionTreeClassifier

dt = DecisionTreeClassifier(criterion = 'gini', random_state = 50)

#Fitting on the training data

dt.fit(X_train, y_train)

#Testing accuracy on the test data

dt.score(X_test, y_test)
```

In the preceding code, we do the following:

1. First, we import `DecisionTreeClassifier` from scikit-learn.

2. We then initialize a `DecisionTreeClassifier` object with two arguments. The first, `criterion`, is the metric with which the tree picks the most important features in a recursive manner, which, in this case, is the Gini coefficient. The second is `random_state`, which is set to 50 so that the model produces the same result every time we run it.

3. Finally, we fit the model on the training data and evaluate its accuracy on the test data.

Hyperparameter tuning for the decision tree

The decision tree has a plethora of hyperparameters that require fine-tuning in order to derive the best possible model that reduces the generalization error as much as possible. In this section, we will focus on two specific hyperparameters:

- **Max depth**: This is the maximum number of children nodes that can grow out from the decision tree until the tree is cut off. For example, if this is set to 3, then the tree will use three children nodes and cut the tree off before it can grow any more.

- **Min samples leaf:** This is the minimum number of samples, or data points, that are required to be present in the leaf node. The leaf node is the last node of the tree. If this parameter is, for example, set to a value of 0.04, it tells the tree that it must grow until the last node contains 4% of the total samples in the data.

In order to optimize the ideal hyperparameter and to extract the best possible decision tree, we use the `GridSearchCV` module from scikit-learn. We can set this up using the following code:

```
from sklearn.model_selection import GridSearchCV

#Creating a grid of different hyperparameters

grid_params = {
    'max_depth': [1,2,3,4,5,6],
    'min_samples_leaf': [0.02,0.04, 0.06, 0.08]
}

#Building a 10 fold Cross Validated GridSearchCV object

grid_object = GridSearchCV(estimator = dt, param_grid = grid_params,
scoring = 'accuracy', cv = 10, n_jobs = -1)
```

In the preceding code, we do the following:

1. We first import the `GridSearchCV` module from scikit-learn.
2. Next, we create a dictionary of possible values for the hyperparameters and store it as `grid_params`.
3. Finally, we create a `GridSearchCV` object with the decision tree classifier as the estimator; that is, the dictionary of hyperparameter values.
4. We set the `scoring` argument as `accuracy`, since we want to extract the accuracy of the best model found by `GridSearchCV`.

We then fit this grid object to the training data using the following code:

```
#Fitting the grid to the training data

grid_object.fit(X_train, y_train)
```

We can then extract the best set of parameters using the following code:

```
#Extracting the best parameters

grid_object.best_params_
```

The output of the preceding code indicates that a maximum depth of 1 and a minimum number of samples at the leaf node of 0.02 are the best parameters for this data. We can use these optimal parameters and construct a new decision tree using the following code:

```
#Extracting the best parameters

grid_object.best_params_
```

Visualizing the decision tree

One of the best aspects of building and implementing a decision tree in order to solve problems is that it can be interpreted quite easily, using a decision tree diagram that explains how the algorithm that you built works. In order to visualize a simple decision tree for the fraud detection dataset, we use the following code:

```
#Package requirements

import pandas as pd
from sklearn.tree import DecisionTreeClassifier
from sklearn.externals.six import StringIO
from IPython.display import Image
from sklearn.tree import export_graphviz
```

```
import pydotplus
from sklearn import tree
```

We start by importing the required packages. The new packages here are the following:

- `StringIO`
- `Image`
- `export_graphviz`
- `pydotplus`
- `tree`

The installations of the packages were covered in `Chapter 1`, *Introducing Machine Learning with scikit-learn*.

Then, we read in the dataset and initialize a decision tree classifier, as shown in the following code:

```
#Reading in the data

df = pd.read_csv('fraud_prediction.csv')
df = df.drop(['Unnamed: 0'], axis = 1)

#Creating the features

features = df.drop('isFraud', axis = 1).values
target = df['isFraud'].values

#Initializing the DT classifier

dt = DecisionTreeClassifier(criterion = 'gini', random_state = 50,
max_depth= 5)
```

Next, we fit the tree on the features and target, and then extract the feature names separately:

```
#Fitting the classifier on the data

dt.fit(features, target)

#Extracting the feature names

feature_names = df.drop('isFraud', axis = 1)
```

We can then visualize the decision tree using the following code:

```
#Creating the tree visualization

data = tree.export_graphviz(dt, out_file=None, feature_names=
feature_names.columns.values, proportion= True)

graph = pydotplus.graph_from_dot_data(data)

# Show graph
Image(graph.create_png())
```

In the preceding code, we do the following:

1. We use the `tree.export_graphviz()` function in order to construct the decision tree object, and store it in a variable called `data`.
2. This function uses a couple of arguments: `dt` is the decision tree that you built; `out_file` is set to `None`, as we do not want to send the tree visualization to any file outside our Jupyter Notebook; the `feature_names` are those we defined earlier; and `proportion` is, set to `True` (this will be explained in more detail later).
3. We then construct a graph of the data contained within the tree so that we can visualize this decision tree graph by using the `pydotplus.graph_from_dot_data()` function on the `data` variable, which contains data about the decision tree.
4. Finally, we visualize the decision tree using the `Image()` function, by passing the graph of the decision tree to it.

This results in a decision tree like that illustrated in the following diagram:

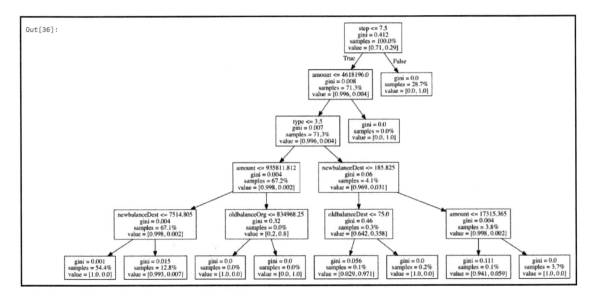

The resultant decision tree

The tree might seem pretty complex to interpret at first, but it's not! In order to interpret this tree, let's consider the root node and the first two children only. This is illustrated in the following diagram:

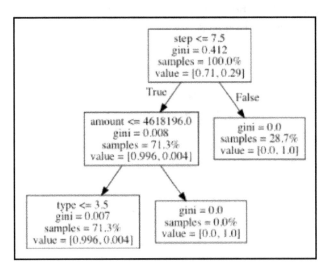

A snippet of the decision tree

In the preceding diagram, note the following:

- In the root node, the tree has identified the 'step' feature as the feature with the highest Gini value.
- The root node makes the split in such a way that 0.71, or 71%, of the data falls into the non-fraudulent transactions, while 0.29, or 29%, of the transactions fall into the fraudulent transactions category.
- If the step is greater than or equal to 7.5 (the right-hand side), then all of the transactions are classified as fraudulent.
- If the step is less than or equal to 7.5 (the left-hand side), then 0.996, or 99.6%, of the transactions are classified as non-fraudulent, while 0.004, or 0.4%, of the transactions are classified as fraudulent.
- If the amount is greater than or equal to 4,618,196.0, then all of the transactions are classified as fraudulent.
- If the amount is less than or equal to 4,618,196.0, then 0.996, or 99.6%, of the transactions are classified as non-fraudulent, while 0.004, or 0.4%, of the transactions are classified as fraudulent.

Note how the decision tree is simply a set of If-then rules, constructed in a nested manner.

The random forests classifier

Now that you understand the core principles of the decision tree at a very foundational level, we will next explore what random forests are. Random forests are a form of *ensemble* learning. An ensemble learning method is one that makes use of multiple machine learning models to make a decision.

Let's consider the following diagram:

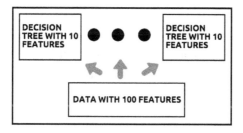

The concept of ensemble learning

The random forest algorithm operates as follows:

1. Assume that you initially have a dataset with 100 features.
2. From this, we will build a decision tree with 10 features initially. The features are selected randomly.
3. Now, using a random selection of the remaining 90 features, we construct the next decision tree, again with 10 features.
4. This process continues until there are no more features left to build a decision tree with.
5. At this point in time, we have 10 decision trees, each with 10 features.
6. Each decision tree is known as the **base estimator** of the random forest.
7. Thus, we have a forest of trees, each built using a random set of 10 features.

The next step for the algorithm is to make the prediction. In order to better understand how the random forest algorithm makes predictions, consider the following diagram:

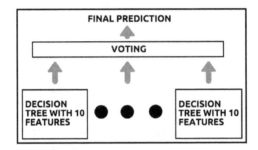

The process of making predictions in random forests

In the preceding diagram, the following occurs:

1. Let's assume that there are 10 decision trees in the random forest.
2. Each decision tree makes a single prediction for the data that comes in.
3. If six trees predict class A, and four trees predict class B, then the final prediction of the random forest algorithm is class A, as it had the majority vote.
4. This process of voting on a prediction, based on the outputs of multiple models, is known as ensemble learning.

Now that you have learned how the algorithm works internally, we can implement it using scikit-learn!

Implementing the random forest classifier in scikit-learn

In this section, we will implement the random forest classifier in scikit-learn. The first step is to read in the data, and split it into training and test sets. This can be done by using the following code:

```
import pandas as pd

#Reading in the dataset

df = pd.read_csv('fraud_prediction.csv')

#Dropping the index

df = df.drop(['Unnamed: 0'], axis = 1)

#Creating the features

features = df.drop('isFraud', axis = 1).values
target = df['isFraud'].values

X_train, X_test, y_train, y_test = train_test_split(features, target,
test_size = 0.3, random_state = 42, stratify = target)
```

The next step is to build the random forest classifier. We can do that using the following code:

```
from sklearn.ensemble import RandomForestClassifier

#Initiliazing an Random Forest Classifier with default parameters

rf_classifier = RandomForestClassifier(random_state = 50)

#Fitting the classifier on the training data

rf_classifier.fit(X_train, y_train)

#Extracting the scores

rf_classifier.score(X_test, y_test)
```

In the preceding code block, we do the following:

1. We first import RandomForestClassifier from scikit-learn.
2. Next, we initialize a random forest classifier model.
3. We then fit this model to our training data, and evaluate its accuracy on the test data.

Hyperparameter tuning for random forest algorithms

In this section, we will learn how to optimize the hyperparameters of the random forest algorithm. Since random forests are fundamentally based on multiple decision trees, the hyperparameters are very similar. In order to optimize the hyperparameters, we use the following code:

```
from sklearn.model_selection import GridSearchCV

#Creating a grid of different hyperparameters

grid_params = {
 'n_estimators': [100,200, 300,400,5000],
 'max_depth': [1,2,4,6,8],
 'min_samples_leaf': [0.05, 0.1, 0.2]
}

#Building a 3 fold Cross-Validated GridSearchCV object

grid_object = GridSearchCV(estimator = rf_classifier, param_grid =
grid_params, scoring = 'accuracy', cv = 3, n_jobs = -1)

#Fitting the grid to the training data

grid_object.fit(X_train, y_train)

#Extracting the best parameters

grid_object.best*params*

#Extracting the best model

rf_best = grid_object.best*estimator_*
```

In the preceding code block, we do the following:

1. We first import the `GridSearchCV` package.
2. We initialize a dictionary of hyperparameter values. The `max_depth` and `min_samples_leaf` values are similar to those of the decision tree.
3. However, `n_estimators` is a new parameter, covering the total number of trees that you want your random forest algorithm to consider while making the final prediction.
4. We then build and fit the `gridsearch` object to the training data and extract the optimal parameters.
5. The best model is then extracted using these optimal hyperparameters.

The AdaBoost classifier

In the section, you will learn how the AdaBoost classifier works internally, and how the concept of boosting might be used to give you better results. Boosting is a form of ensemble machine learning, in which a machine learning model learns from the mistakes of the models that were previously built, thereby increasing its final prediction accuracy.

AdaBoost stands for Adaptive Boosting, and is a boosting algorithm in which a lot of importance is given to the rows of data that the initial predictive model got wrong. This ensures that the next predictive model will not make the same mistakes.

The process by which the AdaBoost algorithm works is illustrated in the following diagram:

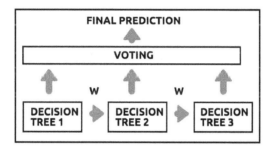

An outline of the AdaBoost algorithm

In the preceding diagram of the AdaBoost algorithm, the following happens:

1. The first decision tree is built and outputs a set of predictions.
2. The predictions that the first decision tree got wrong are given a weight of w. This means that, if the weight is set to 2, then two instances of that particular sample are introduced into the dataset.
3. This enables decision tree 2 to learn at a faster rate, since we have more samples of the data in which an error was made beforehand.
4. This process is repeated until all the trees are built.
5. Finally, the predictions of all the trees are gathered, and a weighted vote is initiated in order to determine the final prediction.

Implementing the AdaBoost classifier in scikit-learn

In this section, we will learn how we can implement the AdaBoost classifier in scikit-learn in order to predict if a transaction is fraudulent or not. As usual, the first step is to import the data and split it into training and testing sets.

This can be done with the following code:

```
#Reading in the dataset

df = pd.read_csv('fraud_prediction.csv')

#Dropping the index

df = df.drop(['Unnamed: 0'], axis = 1)

#Creating the features

features = df.drop('isFraud', axis = 1).values
target = df['isFraud'].values

X_train, X_test, y_train, y_test = train_test_split(features, target,
test_size = 0.3, random_state = 42, stratify = target)
```

The next step is to build the AdaBoost classifier. We can do this using the following code:

```
from sklearn.ensemble import AdaBoostClassifier

#Initialize a tree (Decision Tree with max depth = 1)

tree = DecisionTreeClassifier(max_depth=1, random_state = 42)

#Initialize an AdaBoost classifier with the tree as the base estimator

ada_boost = AdaBoostClassifier(base_estimator = tree, n_estimators=100)

#Fitting the AdaBoost classifier to the training set

ada_boost.fit(X_train, y_train)

#Extracting the accuracy scores from the classifier

ada_boost.score(X_test, y_test)
```

In the preceding code block, we do the following:

1. We first import the `AdaBoostClassifier` package from scikit-learn.
2. Next, we initialize a decision tree that forms the base of our AdaBoost classifier.
3. We then build the AdaBoost classifier, with the base estimator as the decision tree, and we specify that we want 100 decision trees in total.
4. Finally, we fit the classifier to the training data, and extract the accuracy scores from the test data.

Hyperparameter tuning for the AdaBoost classifier

In this section, we will learn how to tune the hyperparameters of the AdaBoost classifier. The AdaBoost classifier has only one parameter of interest—the number of base estimators, or decision trees.

We can optimize the hyperparameters of the AdaBoost classifier using the following code:

```
from sklearn.model_selection import GridSearchCV

#Creating a grid of hyperparameters

grid_params = {
    'n_estimators': [100,200,300]
}

#Building a 3 fold CV GridSearchCV object

grid_object = GridSearchCV(estimator = ada_boost, param_grid = grid_params,
scoring = 'accuracy', cv = 3, n_jobs = -1)

#Fitting the grid to the training data

grid_object.fit(X_train, y_train)

#Extracting the best parameters

grid_object.bestparams

#Extracting the best model

ada_best = grid_object.best_estimator_
```

In the preceding code, we do the following:

1. We first import the `GridSearchCV` package.
2. We initialize a dictionary of hyperparameter values. In this case, `n_estimators` is the number of decision trees.
3. We then build and fit the `gridsearch` object to the training data and extract the best parameters.
4. The best model is then extracted using these optimal hyperparameters.

Regression trees

You have learned how trees are used in order to classify a prediction as belonging to a particular class or category. However, trees can also be used to solve problems related to predicting numeric outcomes. In this section, you will learn about the three types of tree based algorithms that you can implement in scikit-learn in order to predict numeric outcomes, instead of classes:

*   The decision tree regressor
*   The random forest regressor
*   The gradient boosted tree

The decision tree regressor

When we have data that is non-linear in nature, a linear regression model might not be the best model to choose. In such situations, it makes sense to choose a model that can fully capture the non-linearity of such data. A decision tree regressor can be used to predict numeric outcomes, just like that of the linear regression model.

In the case of the decision tree regressor, we use the mean squared error, instead of the Gini metric, in order to determine how the tree is built. You will learn about the mean squared error in detail in `Chapter 8`, *Performance Evaluation Methods*. In a nutshell, the mean squared error is used to tell us about the prediction error rate.

Consider the tree shown in the following diagram:

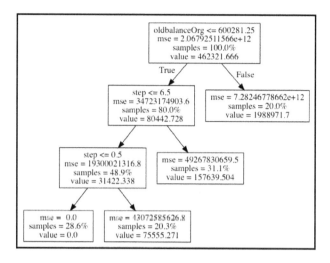

An example decision tree for regression

When considering the preceding diagram of the decision tree, note the following:

- We are trying to predict the amount of a mobile transaction using the tree.
- When the tree tries to decide on a split, it chooses the node in such a way that the target value is closest to the mean values of the target in that node.
- You will notice that, as you go down the tree to the left, along the `True` cases, the mean squared error of the nodes decreases.
- Therefore, the nodes are built in a recursive fashion, such that it reduces the overall mean squared error, thereby obtaining the `True` value.
- In the preceding tree, if the old balance of origination is less than 600,281, then the amount (here, coded as `value`) is 80,442, and if it's greater than 600,281, then the amount is 1,988,971.

Implementing the decision tree regressor in scikit-learn

In this section, you will learn how to implement the decision tree regressor in scikit-learn. The first step is to import the data, and create the features and target variables. We can do this using the following code:

```
import pandas as pd

#Reading in the dataset

df = pd.read_csv('fraud_prediction.csv')

#Dropping the index

df = df.drop(['Unnamed: 0'], axis = 1)

#Creating the features

features = df.drop('amount', axis = 1).values
target = df['amount'].values
```

Note how, in the case of regression, the target variable is the amount, and not the isFraud column.

Next, we split the data into training and test sets, and build the decision tree regressor, as shown in the following code:

```
from sklearn.model_selection import train_test_split
from sklearn.tree import DecisionTreeRegressor

#Splitting the data into training and test sets

X_train, X_test, y_train, y_test = train_test_split(features, target,
test_size = 0.3, random_state = 42)

#Building the decision tree regressor

dt_reg = DecisionTreeRegressor(max_depth = 10, min_samples_leaf = 0.2,
random_state= 50)

#Fitting the tree to the training data

dt_reg.fit(X_train, y_train)
```

In the preceding code, we do the following:

1. We first import the required packages and split the data into training and test sets.
2. Next, we build the decision tree regressor using the `DecisionTreeRegressor()` function.
3. We specify two hyperparameter arguments: `max_depth`, which tells the algorithm how many branches the tree must have, and `min_sample_leaf`, which tells the tree about the minimum number of samples that each node must have. The latter is set to 20%, or 0.2 of the total data, in this case.
4. `random_state` is set to 50 to ensure that the same tree is built every time we run the code.
5. We then fit the tree to the training data.

Visualizing the decision tree regressor

Just as we visualized the decision tree classifier, we can also visualize the decision tree regressor. Instead of showing you the classes or categories to which the node of a tree belongs, you will now be shown the value of the target variable.

We can visualize the decision tree regressor by using the following code:

```
#Package requirements

from sklearn.tree import DecisionTreeClassifier
from sklearn.externals.six import StringIO
from IPython.display import Image
from sklearn.tree import export_graphviz
import pydotplus
from sklearn import tree

#Extracting the feature names

feature_names = df.drop('amount', axis = 1)

#Creating the tree visualization

data = tree.export_graphviz(dt_reg, out_file=None, feature_names=
feature_names.columns.values, proportion= True)

graph = pydotplus.graph_from_dot_data(data)

# Show graph
Image(graph.create_png())
```

The code follows the exact same methodology as that of the decision tree classifier, and will not be discussed in detail here. This produces a decision tree regressor like that in the following diagram:

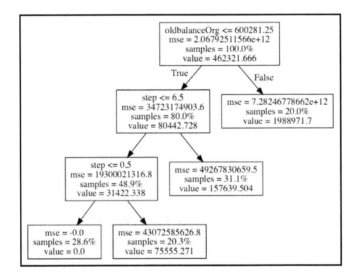

A visualization of the decision tree regressor

The random forest regressor

The random forest regressor takes the decision tree regressor as the base estimator, and makes predictions in a method similar to that of the random forest classifier, as illustrated by the following diagram:

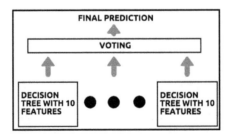

Making the final prediction in the random forest regressor

The only difference between the random forest classifier and the random forest regressor is the fact that, in the case of the latter, the base estimator is a decision tree regressor.

Implementing the random forest regressor in scikit-learn

In this section, you will learn how you can implement the random forest regressor in scikit-learn. The first step is to import the data and split it into training and testing sets. This can be done using the following code:

```
import pandas as pd
from sklearn.model_selection import train_test_split

#Reading in the dataset

df = pd.read_csv('fraud_prediction.csv')

#Dropping the index

df = df.drop(['Unnamed: 0'], axis = 1)

#Creating the features and target arrays

features = df.drop('amount', axis = 1).values
target = df['amount'].values

#Splitting the data into training and test sets

X_train, X_test, y_train, y_test = train_test_split(features, target,
test_size = 0.3, random_state = 42)
```

The next step is to build the random forest regressor. We can do this using the following code:

```
from sklearn.ensemble import RandomForestRegressor

#Initiliazing an Random Forest Regressor with default parameters

rf_reg = RandomForestRegressor(max_depth = 10, min_samples_leaf = 0.2,
random_state = 50)

#Fitting the regressor on the training data

rf_reg.fit(X_train, y_train)
```

In the preceding code, we do the following:

1. We first import the `RandomForestRegressor` module from scikit-learn.
2. We then initialize a random forest regressor object, called `rf_reg`, with a maximum depth of 10 for each decision tree, and the minimum number of data and samples in each tree as 20% of the total data.
3. We then fit the tree to the training set.

The gradient boosted tree

In this section, you will learn how the gradient boosted tree is used for regression, and how you can implement this using scikit-learn.

In the AdaBoost classifier that you learned about earlier in this chapter, weights are added to the examples that the classifier predicted in correctly. In the gradient boosted tree, however, instead of weights, the residual errors are used as labels in each tree in order to make future predictions. This concept is illustrated for you in the following diagram:

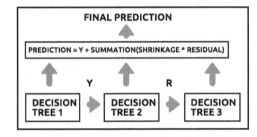

Here is what occurs in the preceding diagram:

1. The first decision tree is trained with the data that you have, and the target variable **Y**.
2. We then compute the residual error for this tree.
3. The residual error is given by the difference between the predicted value and the actual value.
4. The second tree is now trained, using the residuals as the target.
5. This process of building multiple trees is iterative, and continues for the number of base estimators that we have.
6. The final prediction is made by adding the target value predicted by the first tree to the product of the shrinkage and the residuals for all the other trees.

7. The shrinkage is a factor with which we control the rate at which we want this gradient boosting process to take place.

8. A small value of shrinkage (learning rate) implies that the algorithm will learn more quickly, and therefore, must be compensated with a larger number of base estimators (that is, decision trees) in order to prevent overfitting.

9. A larger value of shrinkage (learning rate) implies that the algorithm will learn more slowly, and thus requires fewer trees in order to reduce the computational time.

Implementing the gradient boosted tree in scikit-learn

In this section, we will learn how we can implement the gradient boosted regressor in scikit-learn. The first step, as usual, is to import the dataset, define the features and target arrays, and split the data into training and test sets. This can be done using the following code:

```
import pandas as pd
from sklearn.model_selection import train_test_split

#Reading in the dataset

df = pd.read_csv('fraud_prediction.csv')

#Dropping the index

df = df.drop(['Unnamed: 0'], axis = 1)

#Creating the features

features = df.drop('amount', axis = 1).values
target = df['amount'].values

#Splitting the data into training and test sets

X_train, X_test, y_train, y_test = train_test_split(features, target,
test_size = 0.3, random_state = 42)
```

The next step is to build the gradient boosted regressor. This can be done using the following code:

```
from sklearn.ensemble import GradientBoostingRegressor

#Initializing an Gradient Boosted Regressor with default parameters

gb_reg = GradientBoostingRegressor(max_depth = 5, n_estimators = 100,
```

```
learning_rate = 0.1, random_state = 50)

#Fitting the regressor on the training data

gb_reg.fit(X_train, y_train)
```

In the preceding code, we do the following:

1. We first import `GradientBoostingRegressor` from scikit-learn.
2. We the build a gradient boosted regressor object with three main arguments: the maximum depth of each tree, the total number of trees, and the learning rate.
3. We then fit the regressor on the training data.

Ensemble classifier

The concept of ensemble learning was explored in this chapter, when we learned about random forests, AdaBoost, and gradient boosted trees. However, this concept can be extended to classifiers outside of trees.

If we had built a logistic regression, random forest, and k-nearest neighbors classifiers, and we wanted to group them all together and extract the final prediction through majority voting, then we could do this by using the ensemble classifier.

This concept can be better understood with the aid of the following diagram:

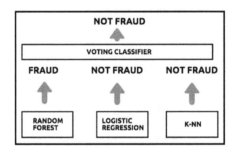

Ensemble learning with a voting classifier to predict fraud transactions

When examining the preceding diagram, note the following:

- The random forest classifier predicted that a particular transaction was fraudulent, while the other two classifiers predicted that the transaction was not fraudulent.
- The voting classifier sees that two out of three (that is, a majority) of the predictions are **Not Fraud**, and hence, outputs the final prediction as **Not Fraud**.

Implementing the voting classifier in scikit-learn

In this section, you will learn how to implement the voting classifier in scikit-learn. The first step is to import the data, create the feature and target arrays, and create the training and testing splits. This can be done using the following code:

```
import pandas as pd
from sklearn.model_selection import train_test_split

#Reading in the dataset

df = pd.read_csv('fraud_prediction.csv')

#Dropping the index

df = df.drop(['Unnamed: 0'], axis = 1)

#Splitting the data into training and test sets

X_train, X_test, y_train, y_test = train_test_split(features, target,
test_size = 0.3, random_state = 42)
```

Next, we will build two classifiers that include the voting classifier: the decision tree classifier and the random forest classifier. This can be done using the following code:

```
from sklearn.tree import DecisionTreeClassifier
from sklearn.ensemble import RandomForestClassifier

#Initializing the DT classifier

dt = DecisionTreeClassifier(criterion = 'gini', random_state = 50)

#Fitting on the training data

dt.fit(X_train, y_train)

#Initiliazing an Random Forest Classifier with default parameters
```

```
rf_classifier = RandomForestClassifier(random_state = 50)

#Fitting the classifier on the training data

rf_classifier.fit(X_train, y_train)
```

Next, we will build the voting classifier by using the following code:

```
from sklearn.ensemble import VotingClassifier

#Creating a list of models

models = [('Decision Tree', dt), ('Random Forest', rf_classifier)]

#Initialize a voting classifier

voting_model = VotingClassifier(estimators = models)

#Fitting the model to the training data

voting_model.fit(X_train, y_train)

#Evaluating the accuracy on the test data

voting_model.score(X_test, y_test)
```

In the preceding code, we do the following:

1. We first import the `VotingClassifier` module from scikit-learn.
2. Next, we create a list of all the models that we want to use in our voting classifier.
3. In the list of classifiers, each model is stored in a tuple, along with the model's name in a string and the model itself.
4. We then initialize a voting classifier with the list of models built in step 2.
5. Finally, the model is fitted to the training data and the accuracy is extracted from the test data.

Summary

While this chapter was rather long, you have entered the world of tree based algorithms, and left with a wide arsenal of tools that you can implement in order to solve both small- and large-scale problems. To summarize, you have learned the following:

- How to use decision trees for classification and regression
- How to use random forests for classification and regression
- How to use AdaBoost for classification
- How to use gradient boosted trees for regression
- How the voting classifier can be used to build a single model out of different models

In the upcoming chapter, you will learn how you can work with data that does not have a target variable or labels, and how to perform unsupervised machine learning in order to solve such problems!

7
Clustering Data with Unsupervised Machine Learning

Most of the data that you will encounter out in the wild will not come with labels. It is impossible to apply supervised machine learning techniques when your data does not come with labels. Unsupervised machine learning addresses this issue by grouping data into clusters; we can then assign labels based on those clusters.

Once the data has been clustered into a specific number of groups, we can proceed to give those groups labels. Unsupervised machine learning is the first step that you, as the data scientist, will have to implement, before you can apply supervised machine learning techniques (such as classification) to make meaningful predictions.

A common application of the unsupervised machine learning algorithm is customer data, which can be found across a wide range of industries. As a data scientist, your job is to find groups of customers that you can segment and deliver targeted products and advertisements to.

In this chapter, you will learn about the following topics:

- The k-means algorithm and how it works internally, in order to cluster unlabeled data
- Implementing the k-means algorithm in scikit-learn
- Using feature engineering to optimize unsupervised machine learning
- Cluster visualization
- Going from unsupervised to supervised machine learning

Technical requirements

You will be required to have Python 3.6 or greater, Pandas ≥ 0.23.4, Scikit-learn ≥ 0.20.0, NumPy ≥ 1.15.1, Matplotlib ≥ 3.0.0, Pydotplus ≥ 2.0.2, Image ≥ 3.1.2, Seaborn ≥ 0.9.0, and SciPy ≥ 1.1.0 installed on your system.

The code files of this chapter can be found on GitHub:
`https://github.com/PacktPublishing/Machine-Learning-with-scikit-learn-Quick-Start-Guide/blob/master/Chapter_07.ipynb`.

Check out the following video to see the code in action:

`http://bit.ly/2qeEJpI`

The k-means algorithm

In this section, you will learn about how the k-means algorithm works under the hood, in order to cluster data into groups that make logical sense.

Let's consider a set of points, as illustrated in the following diagram:

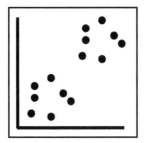

A random set of points

Assignment of centroids

The first step that the algorithm takes is to assign a set of random centroids. Assuming that we want to find two distinct clusters or groups, the algorithm can assign two centroids, as shown in the following diagram:

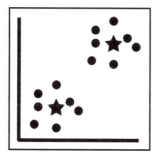

Centroids, represented by stars

In the preceding diagram, the stars represent the centroids of the algorithm. Note that in this case, the clusters' centers perfectly fit the two distinct groups. This is the most ideal case. In reality, the means (or centroids) are assigned randomly, and, with every iteration, the cluster centroids move closer to the center of the two groups.

The algorithm is known as the k-means algorithm, as we try to find the mean of a group of points as the centroid. Since the mean can only be computed for a set of numeric points, such clustering algorithms only work with numerical data.

In reality, the process of grouping these points into two distinct clusters is not this straightforward. A visual representation of the process can be illustrated as follows:

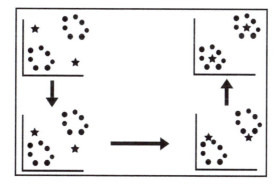

The process of assigning centroids in the k-means algorithm

In the preceding diagram, the process of assigning the random centroids begins in the upper-left corner. As we go down and toward the upper-right corner, note how the centroids move closer to the center of the two distinct groups. In reality, the algorithm does not have an optimal endpoint at which it stops the iteration.

When does the algorithm stop iterating?

Typically, the algorithm looks for two metrics, in order to stop the iteration process:

- The distance between the distinct groups (or clusters) that are formed
- The distance between each point and the centroid of a cluster

The optimal case of cluster formation is when the distance between the distinct groups or clusters are as large as possible, while the distances between each point and the centroid of a cluster are as small as possible.

Implementing the k-means algorithm in scikit-learn

Now that you understand how the k-means algorithm works internally, we can proceed to implement it in scikit-learn. We are going to work with the same fraud detection dataset that we used in all of the previous chapters. The key difference is that we are going to drop the target feature, which contains the labels, and identify the two clusters that are used to detect fraud.

Creating the base k-means model

In order to load the dataset into our workspace and drop the target feature with the labels, we use the following code:

```
import pandas as pd
#Reading in the dataset
df = pd.read_csv('fraud_prediction.csv')
#Dropping the target feature & the index
df = df.drop(['Unnamed: 0', 'isFraud'], axis = 1)
```

Next, we can implement the k-means algorithm with two cluster means. The choice of using two cluster means is arbitrary in nature, since we know that there should be two distinct clusters as a result of two labels: fraud and not fraud transactions. We can do this by using the following code:

```
from sklearn.cluster import KMeans
#Initializing K-means with 2 clusters
k_means = KMeans(n_clusters = 2)
#Fitting the model on the data
k_means.fit(df)
```

In the preceding code, first, we import the KMeans package from scikit-learn and initialize a model with two clusters. We then fit this model to the data by using the `.fit()` function. This results in a set of labels as the output. We can extract the labels by using the following code:

```
#Extracting labels
target_labels = k_means.predict(df)
#Printing the labels
target_labels
```

The output produced by the preceding code is an array of labels for each mobile transaction, as follows:

```
array([0, 0, 0, ..., 1, 0, 1], dtype=int32)
```

Array of labels

Now that we have a set of labels, we know which cluster each transaction falls into. Mobile transactions that have a label of 0 fall into one group, while transactions that have a label of 1 fall into the second group.

The optimal number of clusters

While explaining how the k-means algorithm works, we mentioned how the algorithm terminates once it finds the optimal number of clusters. When picking clusters arbitrarily using scikit-learn, this is not always the case. We need to find the optimal number of clusters, in this case.

One way that we can do this is by a measure known as **inertia.** Inertia measures how close the data points in a cluster are to its centroid. Obviously, a lower inertia signifies that the groups or clusters are tightly packed, which is good.

In order to compute the inertia for the model, we use the following code:

```
# Inertia of present model
k_means.inertia_
```

The preceding code produced an inertia value of *4.99 × 10 ^ 17*, which is extremely large with respect to the other values of inertia produced by different numbers of clusters (explained as follows), and is not a good value of inertia. This suggests that the individual data points are spread out, and are not tightly packed together.

In most cases, we do not really know what the optimal numbers of clusters are, so we need to plot the inertia scores for different numbers of clusters. We can do this by using the following code:

```
import matplotlib.pyplot as plt
import seaborn as sns

#Initialize a list of clusters from 1 to 10 clusters

clusters = [1,2,3,4,5,6,7,8,9,10]

#Create an empty list in order to store the inertia values

inertia_values = []

for cluster in clusters:
    #Build a k-means model for each cluster value
    k_means = KMeans(n_clusters = cluster)
    #Fit the model to the data
    k_means.fit(df)
    # Store inertia value of each model into the empty list
    inertia_values.append(k_means.inertia_)
# Plot the result

plt.lineplot(x = clusters, y = inertia_values)
plt.xlabel('Number of Clusters')
plt.ylabel('Inertia Value')
plt.title('Number of Clusters Vs. Inertia Values')
plt.show()
```

This results in the following plot:

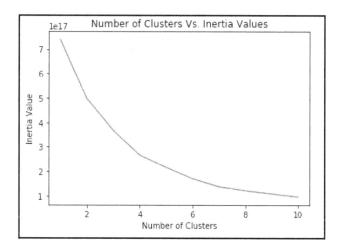

Inertia as a function of the number of clusters

In the preceding code, first, we create a list of clusters that have values from 1 to 10. Each value denotes the number of clusters that will be used in the machine learning model. Next, we create an empty list that will store all of the inertia values that each model will produce.

Next, we loop over the list of clusters and build and evaluate a k-means model for each cluster value in the list. Each model now produces an inertia, which is stored in the list that we initialized at the start of the code block. A simple line plot is then constructed by using the list of clusters along the x axis and the corresponding inertia values along the y axis, using `matplotlib`.

The plot tells us that the inertia values are the lowest when the number of clusters is equal to 10. However, having a large number of clusters is also something that we must aim at avoiding, as having too many groups does not help us to generalize well, and the characteristics about each group become very specific.

Therefore, the ideal way to choose the best number of clusters for a problem, given that we do not have prior information about the number of groups that we want beforehand, is to identify the **elbow point** of the plot.

The elbow point is the point at which the rate of decrease in inertia values slows down. The elbow point is illustrated in the following diagram:

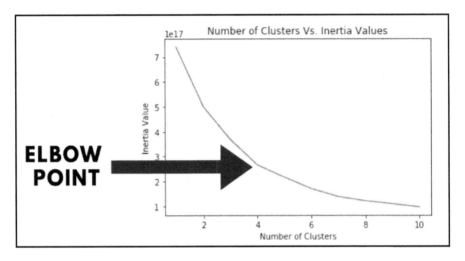

Elbow point of the graph

In the preceding plot, it is clear that the elbow point corresponds to four clusters. This could mean that there are four distinct types of fraudulent transactions, apart from the standard categorizations of fraud and not fraud. However, since we know beforehand that the dataset has a binary target feature with two categories, we will dig too deeply into why four is the ideal number of groups/clusters for this dataset.

Feature engineering for optimization

Engineering the features in your dataset is a concept that is fundamentally used to improve the performance of your model. Fine-tuning the features to the algorithm's design is beneficial, because it can lead to an improvement in accuracy, while reducing the generalization errors at the same time. The different kinds of feature engineering techniques for optimizing your dataset that you will learn are as follows:

- Scaling
- Principal component analysis

Scaling

Scaling is the process of standardizing your data so that the values under every feature fall within a certain range, such as -1 to +1. In order to scale the data, we subtract each value of a particular feature with the mean of that feature, and divide it by the variance of that feature. In order to scale the features in our fraud detection dataset, we use the following code:

```
from sklearn.preprocessing import StandardScaler

#Setting up the standard scaler

scale_data = StandardScaler()

#Scaling the data

scale_data.fit(df)

df_scaled = scale_data.transform(df)

#Applying the K-Means algorithm on the scaled data

#Initializing K-means with 2 clusters

k_means = KMeans(n_clusters = 2)

#Fitting the model on the data

k_means.fit(df_scaled)

# Inertia of present model

k_means.inertia_
```

In the preceding code, we use the `StandardScalar()` function to scale our dataframe, and then we build a k-means model with two clusters on the scaled data. After evaluating the inertia of the model, the value output is 295,000, which is substantially better than the value of 4.99×10^{17}, produced by the model without scaling.

We can then create a new plot of the number of clusters versus the inertia values, using the same code that we did earlier, with the only difference being replacing the original dataframe with the scaled dataframe:

```
#Initialize a list of clusters from 1 to 10 clusters

clusters = [1,2,3,4,5,6,7,8,9,10]

#Create an empty list in order to store the inertia values

inertia_values = []

for cluster in clusters:
    #Build a k-means model for each cluster value
    k_means = KMeans(n_clusters = cluster)
    #Fit the model to the data
    k_means.fit(df_scaled)
    # Store inertia value of each model into the empty list
    inertia_values.append(k_means.inertia_)
# Plot the result

sns.lineplot(x = clusters, y = inertia_values)
plt.xlabel('Number of Clusters')
plt.ylabel('Inertia Value')
plt.title('Number of Clusters Vs. Inertia Values')
plt.show()
```

This produces the following output:

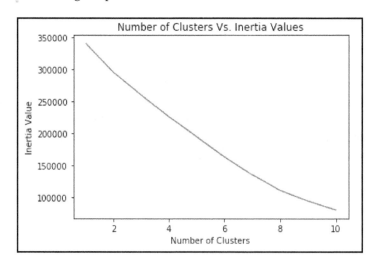

Optimal number of clusters, post-scaling

We notice that the preceding plot does not have a very clear elbow point, where the rate of decrease in the inertia values is lower. However, if we look closely, we can find this point at **8** clusters.

Principal component analysis

The **principal component analysis** (**PCA**) is a subset of dimensionality reduction. **Dimensionality reduction** is the process of reducing the number of features that provide no predictive value to a predictive model. We also optimize and improve the computational efficiency of processing the algorithms. This is because a dataset with a smaller number of features will make it easier for the algorithm to detect patterns more quickly.

The first step in PCA is called **decorrelation**. Features that are highly correlated with each other provide no value to the predictive model. Therefore, in the decorrelation step, the PCA takes two highly correlated features and spreads their data points such that it's aligned across the axis, and is not correlated anymore. This process can be illustrated as follows:

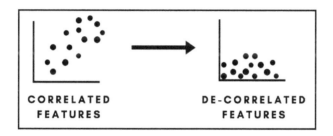

The process of decorrelation

Once the features are decorrelated, the principal components (or features) are extracted from the data. These features are the ones that have high variance, and, in turn, provide the most value to a predictive model. The features with low variance are discarded, and thus, the number of dimensions in the dataset is reduced.

In order to perform dimensionality reduction using PCA, we use the following code:

```
from sklearn.decomposition import PCA

#Initialize a PCA model with 5 features

pca_model = PCA(n_components = 5)
```

```
#Fit the model to the scaled dataframe

pca_model.fit(df_scaled)

#Transform the features so that it is de-correlated

pca_transform = pca_model.transform(df_scaled)

#Check to see if there are only 5 features

pca_transform.shape
```

In the preceding code, first, we import the PCA method from scikit-learn. Next, we initialize a PCA model with five components. Here, we are specifying that we want the PCA to reduce the dataset to only the five most important features.

We then fit the PCA model to the dataframe and transform it, in order to obtain the decorrelated features. Checking the shape of the final array of features, we can see that it only has five features. Finally, we create a new k-means model with only the principal component features, as shown in the following code:

```
#Applying the K-Means algorithm on the scaled data

#Initializing K-means with 2 clusters

k_means = KMeans(n_clusters = 2)#Fitting the model on the data

k_means.fit(pca_transform)

# Inertia of present model

k_means.inertia_
```

Evaluating the inertia of the new model improved its performance. We obtained a lower value of inertia than in the case of the scaled model. Now, let's evaluate the inertia scores for different numbers of principal components or features. In order to this, we use the following code:

```
#Initialize a list of principal components

components = [1,2,3,4,5,6,7,8,9,10]

#Create an empty list in order to store the inertia values

inertia_values = []

for comp in components:
```

```
#Initialize a PCA model

pca_model = PCA(n_components = comp)
#Fit the model to the dataframe

pca_model.fit(df_scaled)
#Transform the features so that it is de-correlated

pca_transform = pca_model.transform(df_scaled)
#Build a k-means model
k_means = KMeans(n_clusters = 2)
#Fit the model to the data
k_means.fit(pca_transform)
# Store inertia value of each model into the empty list
inertia_values.append(k_means.inertia_)
# Plot the result

sns.lineplot(x = components, y = inertia_values)
plt.xlabel('Number of Principal Components')
plt.ylabel('Inertia Value')
plt.title('Number of Components Vs. Inertia Values')
plt.show()
```

In the preceding code, the following applies:

1. First, we initialize a list to store the different principal component values that we want to build our models with. These values are from 1 to 10.
2. Next, we initialize an empty list, in order to store the inertia values from each and every model.
3. Using each principal component value, we build a new k-means model and append the inertia value for that model into the empty list.
4. Finally, a plot is constructed between the inertia values and the different values of components.

This plot is illustrated as follows:

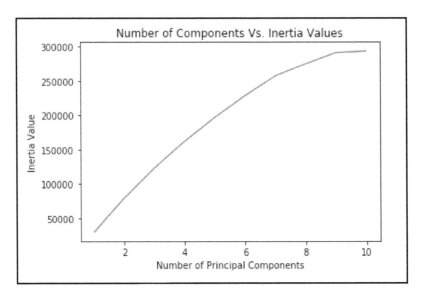

Inertia values versus the numbers of principal components

In the preceding plot, it is clear that the inertia value is lowest for one component.

Cluster visualization

Visualizing how your clusters are formed is no easy task when the number of variables/dimensions in your dataset is very large. There are two main methods that you can use in order to visualize how the clusters are distributed, as follows:

- **t-SNE**: This creates a map of the dataset in two-dimensional space
- **Hierarchical clustering**: This uses a tree-based visualization, known as a **dendrogram**, in order to create hierarchies

In this section, you will learn how to implement these visualization techniques, in order to create compelling cluster visuals.

t-SNE

The **t-SNE** is an abbreviation that stands for **t-distributed stochastic neighbor embedding**. The fundamental concept behind the t-SNE is to map a higher dimension to a two-dimensional space. In simple terms, if your dataset has more than two features, the t-SNE does a great job at showing you how your entire dataset can be visualized on your computer screen!

The first step is to implement the k-means algorithm and create a set of prediction labels that we can merge into the unlabeled dataset. We can do this by using the following code:

```
#Reading in the dataset

df = pd.read_csv('fraud_prediction.csv')

#Dropping the target feature & the index

df = df.drop(['Unnamed: 0', 'isFraud'], axis = 1)

#Initializing K-means with 2 clusters

k_means = KMeans(n_clusters = 2)

#Fitting the model on the data

k_means.fit(df)

#Extracting labels

target_labels = k_means.predict(df)

#Converting the labels to a series

target_labels = pd.Series(target_labels)

#Merging the labels to the dataset

df = pd.merge(df, pd.DataFrame(target_labels), left_index=True,
right_index=True)

#Renaming the target

df['fraud'] = df[0]
df = df.drop([0], axis = 1)
```

Don't worry about how the preceding segment of code works for the moment, as this will be explained in detail in a later section within this chapter, when we deal with converting an unsupervised machine learning problem into a supervised learning one.

Next, we will create a t-SNE object and fit that into our array of data points that consists of only the features. We will then transform the features at the same time so that we can view all the features on a two-dimensional space. This is done in the following code segment:

```
from sklearn.manifold import TSNE

#Creating the features

features = df.drop('fraud', axis = 1).values

target = df['fraud'].values

#Initialize a TSNE object

tsne_object = TSNE()

#Fit and transform the features using the TSNE object

transformed = tsne_object.fit_transform(features)
```

In the preceding code, the following applies:

1. First, we initialize the t-SNE object by using the `TSNE()` function.
2. Using the t-SNE object, we fit and transform the data in our features, using the `fit_transform()` method.

Next, we create the t-SNE visualization by using the following code:

```
#Creating a t-SNE visualization

x_axis = transformed[:,0]


y_axis = transformed[:,1]


plt.scatter(x_axis, y_axis, c = target)

plt.show()
```

In the preceding code, the following applies:

1. We extract the first and second features from the set of transformed features for the x axis and *y* axis, respectively.
2. We then plot a scatter plot and color it by the target labels, which were generated earlier, using the k-means algorithm. This generates the following plot:

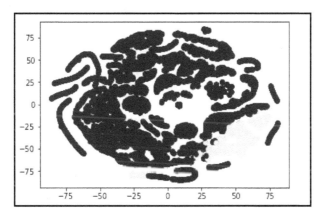

t-SNE visualization

In the preceding plot, the yellow color represents the transactions that have been assigned the fraud label, while the purple color represents the transactions that have been assigned the non-fraudulent label. (Please refer to the color version of the image.)

Hierarchical clustering

As discussed initially, the hierarchical clustering technique uses the dendrogram to visualize clusters or groups. In order to explain how the dendrogram works, we will consider a dataset with four features.

Step 1 – Individual features as individual clusters

In the first step, each feature in the dataset is considered to be its own cluster. This is illustrated in the following diagram:

Each feature as a single cluster in the dendrogram

Each feature in the preceding diagram is one single cluster, at this point in time. The algorithm now searches to find the two features that are closest to each other, and merges them into a single cluster.

Step 2 – The merge

In this step, the algorithm merges the data points in the two closest features together, into one single cluster. This is illustrated in the following diagram:

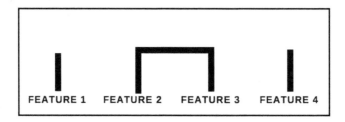

The process in which features merge into a single cluster

In the preceding diagram, it is clear that the algorithm has now chosen **Feature 2** and **Feature 3**, and has decided that the data under these two features are the closest to each other.

Step 3 – Iteration

The algorithm now continues the process of merging features together iteratively, until no more clusters can be formed. The final dendrogram that is formed is as follows:

In the preceding diagram, **Feature 2** and **Feature 3** were grouped into a single cluster. The algorithm then decided that **Feature 1** and the cluster of **Feature 2** and **3** were closest to each other. Therefore, these three features were clustered into one group. Finally, **Feature 4** was grouped together with **Feature 3**.

Implementing hierarchical clustering

Now that you have learned how hierarchical clustering works, we can implement this concept. In order to create a hierarchical cluster, we use the following code:

```
from scipy.cluster.hierarchy import linkage
from scipy.cluster.hierarchy import dendrogram
import numpy as np
import matplotlib.pyplot as plt

#Creating an array of 4 features

array = np.array([[1,2,3,4], [5,6,7,8], [2,3,4,5], [5,6,4,3]])

feature_names = ['a', 'b', 'c', 'd']

#Creating clusters

clusters = linkage(array, method = 'complete')

#Creating a dendrogram

dendrogram(clusters, labels = feature_names, leaf_rotation = 90)

plt.show()
```

The preceding code results in a dendrogram, as illustrated in the following diagram:

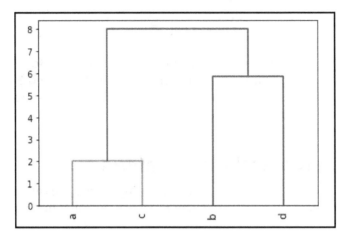

Dendrogram

In the preceding code, the following applies:

1. First, we create an array with four columns.
2. We then use the `linkage` function to create the clusters. Within the function, we specify the `method` argument as complete, in order to indicate that we want the entire dendrogram.
3. Finally, we use the `dendrogram` function to create the dendrogram with the clusters. We set the label names to the list of feature names that was created earlier in the code.

Going from unsupervised to supervised learning

The eventual goal of unsupervised learning is to take a dataset with no labels and assign labels to each row of the dataset, so that we can run a supervised learning algorithm through it. This allows us to create predictions that make use of the labels.

In this section, you will learn how to convert the labels generated by the unsupervised machine learning algorithm into a decision tree that makes use of those labels.

Creating a labeled dataset

The first step is to convert the labels generated by an unsupervised machine learning algorithm, such as the k-means algorithm, and append it to the dataset. We can do this by using the following code:

```
#Reading in the dataset

df = pd.read_csv('fraud_prediction.csv')

#Dropping the target feature & the index

df = df.drop(['Unnamed: 0', 'isFraud'], axis = 1)
```

In the preceding code, we read in the fraud detection dataset and drop the target and index columns:

```
#Initializing K-means with 2 clusters

k_means = KMeans(n_clusters = 2)

#Fitting the model on the data

k_means.fit(df)
```

Next, in the preceding code we initialize and fit a k-means model with two clusters:

```
#Extracting labels

target_labels = k_means.predict(df)

#Converting the labels to a series

target_labels = pd.Series(target_labels)

#Merging the labels to the dataset

df = pd.merge(df, pd.DataFrame(target_labels), left_index=True,
right_index=True)
```

Finally, we create the target labels by using the `predict()` method, and convert it into a `pandas` series. We then merge this series into the dataframe, in order to create our labeled dataset.

Building the decision tree

Now that we have the labeled dataset, we can create a decision tree, in order to convert the unsupervised machine learning problem into a supervised machine learning one.

In order to do this, we start with all of the necessary package imports, as shown in the following code:

```
from sklearn.tree import DecisionTreeClassifier
from sklearn.externals.six import StringIO
from IPython.display import Image
from sklearn.tree import export_graphviz
import pydotplus
from sklearn import tree
```

Next, we rename the target column to a name that is appropriate (when we merged the target labels created by the k-means algorithm, it produced 0 as the default name). We can do this by using the following code:

```
#Renaming the target

df['fraud'] = df[0]
df = df.drop([0], axis = 1)
```

Next, we build the decision tree classification algorithm, using the following code:

```
#Creating the features

features = df.drop('fraud', axis = 1).values

target = df['fraud'].values

#Initializing an empty DT classifier with a random state value of 42

dt_classifier = DecisionTreeClassifier(criterion = 'gini', random_state = 42)

#Fitting the classifier on the training data

dt_classifier.fit(features, target)
```

In the preceding code, first, we create the features and target variables and initialize a decision tree classifier. We then fit the classifier onto the features and target.

Finally, we want to visualize the decision tree. We can do this by using the following code:

```
#Creating a data frame with the features only

features = df.drop('fraud', axis = 1)

dot_data = tree.export_graphviz(dt_classifier, out_file=None,
feature_names= features.columns)

# Draw graph

graph = pydotplus.graph_from_dot_data(dot_data)

#Show graph

Image(graph.create_png())
```

This results in the decision tree shown in the following diagram:

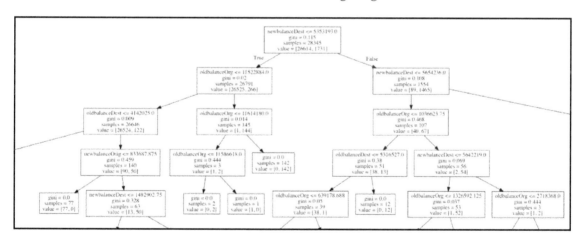

A part of the decision tree that was created

Summary

In this chapter, you learned about how the k-means algorithm works, in order to cluster unlabeled data points into clusters or groups. You then learned how to implement the same using scikit-learn, and we expanded upon the feature engineering aspect of the implementation.

Having learned how to visualize clusters using hierarchical clustering and t-SNE, you then learned how to map a multi-dimensional dataset into a two-dimensional space. Finally, you learned how to convert an unsupervised machine learning problem into a supervised learning one, using decision trees.

In the next (and final) chapter, you will learn how to formally evaluate the performance of all of the machine learning algorithms that you have built so far!

8
Performance Evaluation Methods

Your method of performance evaluation will vary by the type of machine learning algorithm that you choose to implement. In general, there are different metrics that can potentially determine how well your model is performing at its given task for classification, regression, and unsupervised machine learning algorithms.

In this chapter, we will explore how the different performance evaluation methods can help you to better understand your model. The chapter will be split into three sections, as follows:

- Performance evaluation for classification algorithms
- Performance evaluation for regression algorithms
- Performance evaluation for unsupervised algorithms

Technical requirements

You will be required to have Python 3.6 or greater, Pandas ≥ 0.23.4, Scikit-learn ≥ 0.20.0, NumPy ≥ 1.15.1, Matplotlib ≥ 3.0.0, and Scikit-plot ≥ 0.3.7 installed on your system.

The code files of this chapter can be found on GitHub:
`https://github.com/PacktPublishing/Machine-Learning-with-scikit-learn-Quick-Start-Guide/blob/master/Chapter_08.ipynb`

Check out the following video to see the code in action:

`http://bit.ly/2EY4nJU`

Why is performance evaluation critical?

It is key for you to understand why we need to evaluate the performance of a model in the first place. Some of the potential reasons why performance evaluation is critical are as follows:

- **It prevents overfitting**: Overfitting occurs when your algorithm hugs the data too tightly and makes predictions that are specific to only one dataset. In other words, your model cannot generalize its predictions outside of the data that it was trained on.
- **It prevents underfitting**: This is the exact opposite of overfitting. In this case, the model is very generic in nature.
- **Understanding predictions**: Performance evaluation methods will help you to understand, in greater detail, how your model makes predictions, along with the nature of those predictions and other useful information, such as the accuracy of your model.

Performance evaluation for classification algorithms

In order to evaluate the performance of classification, let's consider the two classification algorithms that we have built in this book: k-nearest neighbors and logistic regression.

The first step will be to implement both of these algorithms in the fraud detection dataset. We can do this by using the following code:

```
import pandas as pd
from sklearn.model_selection import train_test_split
from sklearn.neighbors import KNeighborsClassifier
from sklearn import linear_model

#Reading in the fraud detection dataset

df = pd.read_csv('fraud_prediction.csv')

#Creating the features

features = df.drop('isFraud', axis = 1).values
target = df['isFraud'].values

#Splitting the data into training and test sets
```

```
X_train, X_test, y_train, y_test = train_test_split(features, target,
test_size = 0.3, random_state = 42, stratify = target)

# Building the K-NN Classifier

knn_classifier = KNeighborsClassifier(n_neighbors=3)

knn_classifier.fit(X_train, y_train)

#Initializing an logistic regression object

logistic_regression = linear_model.LogisticRegression()

#Fitting the model to the training and test sets

logistic_regression.fit(X_train, y_train)
```

In the preceding code, we read the fraud detection dataset into our notebook and split the data into the features and target variables, as usual. We then split the data into training and test sets, and build the k-nearest neighbors and logistic regression models in the training data.

In this section, you will learn how to evaluate the performance of a single model: k-nearest neighbors. You will also learn how to compare and contrast multiple models. Therefore, you will learn about the following things:

- Confusion matrix
- Normalized confusion matrix
- Area under the curve (auc score)
- Cumulative gains curve
- Lift curve
- K-S statistic plot
- Calibration plot
- Learning curve
- Cross-validated box plot

Some of the visualizations in this section will require a package titled scikit-plot. The scikit-plot package is very effective, and it is used to visualize the various performance measures of machine learning models. It was specifically made for models that are built using scikit-learn.

In order to install `scikit-plot` on your local machine, using `pip` in Terminal, we use the following code:

```
pip3 install scikit-plot
```

If you are using the Anaconda distribution to manage your Python packages, you can install `scikit-plot` by using the following code:

```
conda install -c conda-forge scikit-plot
```

The confusion matrix

Until now, we have used the accuracy as the sole measure of model performance. That was fine, because we have a balanced dataset. A balanced dataset is a dataset in which there are almost the same numbers of labels for each category. In the dataset that we are working with, 8,000 labels belong to the fraudulent transactions, while 12,000 belong to the non-fraudulent transactions.

Imagine a situation in which 90% of our data had non-fraudulent transactions, while only 10% of the transactions had fraudulent cases. If the classifier reported an accuracy of 90%, it wouldn't make sense, because most of the data that it has seen thus far were the non-fraudulent cases and it has seen very little of the fraudulent cases. So, even if it classified 90% of the cases accurately, it would mean that most of the cases that it classified would belong to the non-fraudulent cases. That would provide no value to us.

A **confusion matrix** is a performance evaluation technique that can be used in such cases, which do not involve a balanced dataset. The confusion matrix for our dataset would look as follows:

	PREDICTED: FRAUD	**PREDICTED: NOT FRAUD**
ACTUAL: FRAUD	**TRUE POSITIVE**	**FALSE NEGATIVE**
ACTUAL: NOT FRAUD	**FALSE POSITIVE**	**TRUE NEGATIVE**

Confusion matrix for fraudulent transactions

The goal of the confusion matrix is to maximize the number of true positives and true negatives, as this gives the correct predictions; it also minimizes the number of false negatives and false positives, as they give us the wrong predictions.

Depending on your problem, the false positives might be more problematic than the false negatives (and vice versa), and thus, the goal of building the right classifier should be to solve your problem in the best possible way.

In order to implement the confusion matrix in scikit-learn, we use the following code:

```
from sklearn.metrics import confusion_matrix

#Creating predictions on the test set

prediction = knn_classifier.predict(X_test)

#Creating the confusion matrix

print(confusion_matrix(y_test, prediction))
```

This produces the following output:

```
[[6026   14]
 [  32 2432]]
```

The confusion matrix output from our classifier for fraudulent transactions

In the preceding code, we create a set of predictions using the .predict() method on the test training data, and then we use the confusion_matrix() function on the test set of the target variable and the predictions that were created earlier.

The preceding confusion matrix looks almost perfect, as most cases are classified into the true positive and true negative categories, along the main diagonal. Only 46 cases are classified incorrectly, and this number is almost equal. This means that the numbers of false positives and false negatives are minimal and balanced, and one does not outweigh the other. This is an example of the ideal classifier.

Three other metrics that can be derived from the confusion matrix are **precision**, **recall**, and **F1-score**. A high value of precision indicates that not many non-fraudulent transactions are classified as fraudulent, while a high value of recall indicates that most of the fraudulent cases were predicted correctly.

The F1-score is the weighted average of the precision and recall.

We can compute the precision and recall by using the following code:

```
from sklearn.metrics import classification_report

#Creating the classification report

print(classification_report(y_test, prediction))
```

This produces the following output:

```
              precision    recall  f1-score   support

         0.0       0.99      1.00      1.00      6040
         1.0       0.99      0.99      0.99      2464

avg / total       0.99      0.99      0.99      8504
```

Classification report

In the preceding code, we use the `classificiation_report()` function with two arguments: the test set of the target variable and the prediction variable that we created for the confusion matrix earlier.

In the output, the precision, recall, and F1-score are all high, because we have built the ideal machine learning model. These values range from 0 to 1, with 1 being the highest.

The normalized confusion matrix

A **normalized confusion matrix** makes it easier for the data scientist to visually interpret how the labels are being predicted. In order to construct a normalized confusion matrix, we use the following code:

```
import matplotlib.pyplot as plt
import scikitplot as skplt

#Normalized confusion matrix for the K-NN model

prediction_labels = knn_classifier.predict(X_test)
skplt.metrics.plot_confusion_matrix(y_test, prediction_labels,
normalize=True)
plt.show()
```

This results in the following normalized confusion matrix:

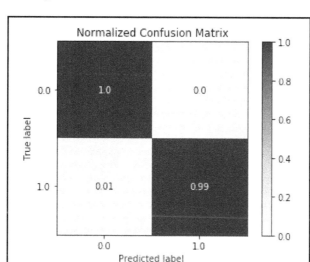

Normalized confusion matrix for the K-NN model

In the preceding plot, the predicted labels are along the *x* axis, while the true (or actual) labels are along the *y* axis. We can see that the model has 0.01, or 1%, of the predictions for the fraudulent transactions incorrect, while 0.99, or 99%, of the fraudulent transactions have been predicted correctly. We can also see that the K-NN model predicted 100% of the non-fraudulent transactions correctly.

Now, we can compare the performance of the logistic regression model by using a normalized confusion matrix, as follows:

```
#Normalized confusion matrix for the logistic regression model

prediction_labels = logistic_regression.predict(X_test)
skplt.metrics.plot_confusion_matrix(y_test, prediction_labels,
normalize=True)
plt.show()
```

This results in the following normalized confusion matrix:

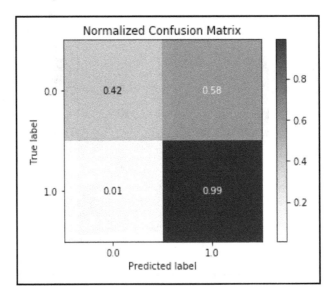

Normalized confusion matrix for the logistic regression model

In the preceding confusion matrix, it is clear that the logistic regression model only predicted 42% of the non-fraudulent transactions correctly. This indicates, almost instantly, that the k-nearest neighbor model performed better.

Area under the curve

The curve, in this case, is the **receiver operator characteristics (ROC)** curve. This is a plot between the true positive rate and the false positive rate. We can plot this curve as follows:

```
from sklearn.metrics import roc_curve
from sklearn.metrics import roc_auc_score
import matplotlib.pyplot as plt

#Probabilities for each prediction output

target_prob = knn_classifier.predict_proba(X_test)[:,1]

#Plotting the ROC curve

fpr, tpr, thresholds = roc_curve(y_test, target_prob)

plt.plot([0,1], [0,1], 'k--')
```

```
plt.plot(fpr, tpr)

plt.xlabel('False Positive Rate')

plt.ylabel('True Positive Rate')

plt.title('ROC Curve')

plt.show()
```

This produces the following curve:

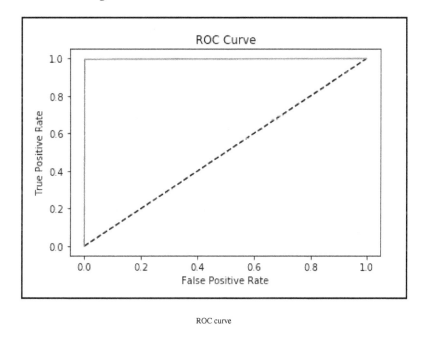

ROC curve

In the preceding code, first, we create a set of probabilities for each of the predicted labels. For instance, the predicted label of **1** would have a certain set of probabilities associated with it, while the label **0** would have a certain set of probabilities associated with it. Using these probabilities, we use the `roc_curve()` function, along with the target test set, to generate the ROC curve.

The preceding curve is an example of a perfect ROC curve. The preceding curve has a true positive rate of 1.0, which indicates accurate predictions, while it has a false positive rate of 0, which indicates a lack of wrong predictions.

Such a curve also has the most area under the curve, as compared to the curves of models that have a lower accuracy. In order to compute the area under the curve score, we use the following code:

```
#Computing the auc score

roc_auc_score(y_test, target_prob)
```

This produces a score of 0.99. A higher auc score indicates a better performing model.

Cumulative gains curve

When building multiple machine learning models, it is important to understand which of the models in question produces the type of predictions that you want it to generate. The **cumulative gains curve** helps you with the process of model comparison, by telling you about the percentage of a category/class that appears within a percentage of the sample population for a particular model.

In simple terms, in the fraud detection dataset, we might want to pick a model that can predict a larger number of fraudulent transactions, as opposed to a model that cannot. In order to construct the cumulative gains plot for the k-nearest neighbors model, we use the following code:

```
import scikitplot as skplt

target_prob = knn_classifier.predict_proba(X_test)
skplt.metrics.plot_cumulative_gain(y_test, target_prob)
plt.show()
```

This results in the following plot:

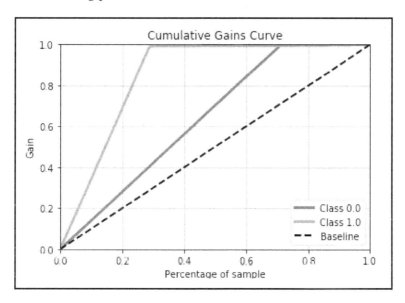

Cumulative gains plot for the k-nearest neighbors model

In the preceding code, the following applies:

- First, we import the scikit-plot package, which generates the preceding plot. We then compute the probabilities for the target variable, which, in this case, are the probabilities if a particular mobile transaction is fraudulent or not on the test data.
- Finally, we use the plot_cumulative_gain() function on these probabilities and the test data target labels, in order to generate the preceding plot.

How do we interpret the preceding plot? We simply look for the point at which a certain percentage of the data contains 100% of the target class. This is illustrated in the following diagram:

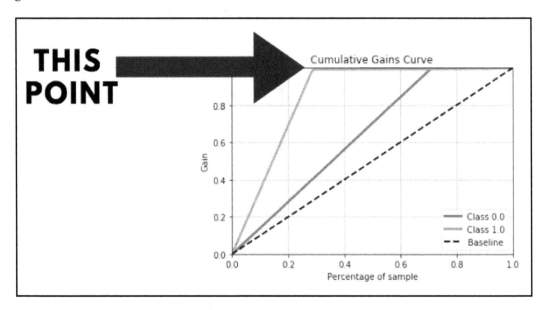

Point at which 100% of the target class exists

The point defined in the preceding diagram corresponds to a value of 0.3 on the x axis and 1.0 on the y axis. This means that 0.3 to 1.0 (or 30% to 100%) of the data will consist of the target class, 1, which are the fraudulent transactions.

This can also be interpreted as follows: 70% of the total data will contain 100% of the fraudulent transaction predictions if you use the k-nearest neighbors model.

Now, let's compute the cumulative gains curve for the logistic regression model, and see if it is different. In order to do this, we use the following code:

```
#Cumulative gains plot for the logistic regression model

target_prob = logistic_regression.predict_proba(X_test)
skplt.metrics.plot_cumulative_gain(y_test, target_prob)
plt.show()
```

This results in the following plot:

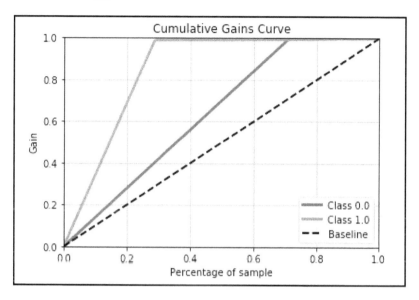

Cumulative gains plot for the logistic regression model

The preceding plot is similar to the cumulative gains plot that was previously produced by the K-NN model, in that 70% of the data contains 100% of the target class. Therefore, using either the K-NN or the logistic regression model will yield similar results.

However, it is a good practice to compare how different models behave by using the cumulative gains chart, in order to gain a fundamental understanding of how your model makes predictions.

Lift curve

A **lift curve** gives you information about how well you can make predictions by using a machine learning model, as opposed to when you are not using one. In order to construct a lift curve for the k-nearest neighbor model, we use the following code:

```
# Lift curve for the K-NN model

target_prob = knn_classifier.predict_proba(X_test)
skplt.metrics.plot_lift_curve(y_test, target_prob)
plt.show()
```

This results in the following plot:

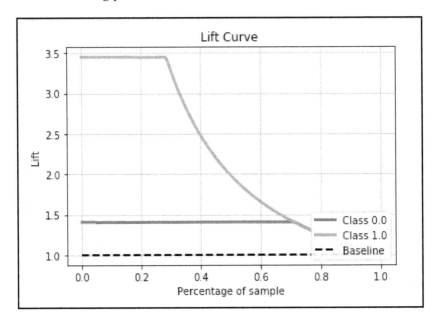

Lift curve for the K-NN model

How do we interpret the preceding lift curve? We have to look for the point at which the curve dips. This is illustrated for you in the following diagram:

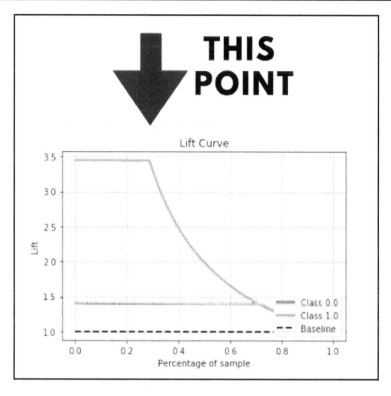

Point of interest in the lift curve

In the preceding plot, the point that is highlighted is the point that we want to look for in any lift curve. The point tells us that 0.3, or 30%, of our total data will perform 3.5 times better when using the K-NN predictive model, as opposed to when we do not use any model at all to predict the fraudulent transactions.

Now, we can construct the lift curve for the logistic regression model, in order to compare and contrast the performance of the two models. We can do this by using the following code:

```
#Cumulative gains plot for the logistic regression model

target_prob = logistic_regression.predict_proba(X_test)
skplt.metrics.plot_lift_curve(y_test, target_prob)
plt.show()
```

This results in the following plot:

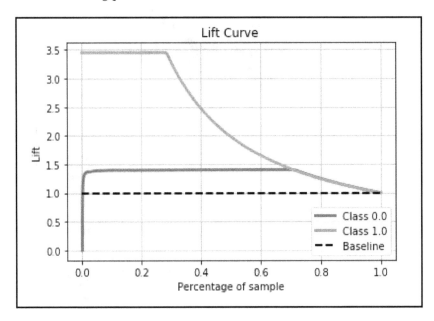

Lift curve for the logistic regression model

Although the plot tells us that 30% of the data will see an improved performance (similar to that of the K-NN model that we built earlier in order to predict the fraudulent transactions), there is a difference when it comes to predicting the non-fraudulent transactions (the blue line).

For a small percentage of the data, the lift curve for the non-fraudulent transactions is actually lower than the baseline (the dotted line). This means that the logistic regression model does worse than not using a predictive model for a small percentage of the data when it comes to predicting the non-fraudulent transactions.

K-S statistic plot

The **K-S statistic plot**, or the **Kolmogorov Smirnov** statistic plot, is a plot that tells you whether the model gets confused when it comes to predicting the different labels in your dataset. In order to illustrate what the term *confused* means in this case, we will construct the K-S statistic plot for the K-NN model by using the following code:

```
#KS plot for the K-NN model

target_proba = knn_classifier.predict_proba(X_test)
skplt.metrics.plot_ks_statistic(y_test, target_proba)
plt.show()
```

This results in the following plot:

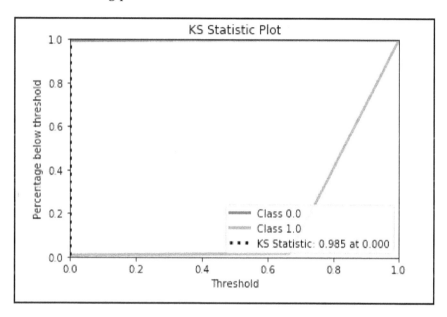

K-S statistic plot for the K-NN model

In the preceding plot, the following applies:

- The dotted line is the distance between the predictions for the fraudulent transactions (the yellow line at the bottom) and the non-fraudulent transactions (the blue line at the top). This distance is 0.985, as indicated by the plot.
- A K-S statistic score that is close to 1 is usually a good indication that the model does not get confused between predicting the two different target labels, and can make a clear distinction when it comes to predicting the labels.
- In the preceding plot, the score of 0.985 can be observed as the difference between the two classes of predictions, for up to 70% (0.7) of the data. This can be observed along the *x* axis, as a threshold of 0.7 still has the maximum separation distance.

We can now compute the K-S statistic plot for the logistic regression model, in order to compare which of the two models provides a better distinction in predictions between the two class labels. We can do this by using the following code:

```
#KS plot for the logistic regression model

target_proba = logistic_regression.predict_proba(X_test)
skplt.metrics.plot_ks_statistic(y_test, target_proba)
plt.show()
```

This results in the following plot:

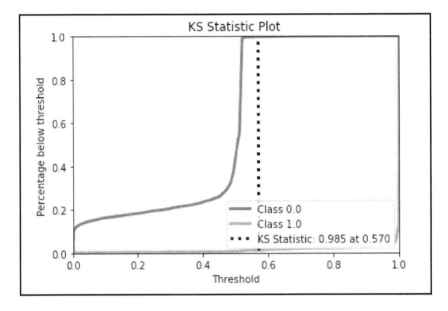

K-S statistic plot for the logistic regression model

Although the two models have the same separation score of 0.985, the threshold at which the separation occurs is quite different. In the case of logistic regression, this distance only occurs for the bottom 43% of the data, since the maximum separation starts at a threshold of 0.57, along the *x* axis.

This means that the k-nearest neighbors model, which has a large distance for about 70% of the total data, is much better at making predictions about fraudulent transactions.

Calibration plot

A **calibration plot**, as the name suggests, tells you how well calibrated your model is. A well-calibrated model will have a prediction score equal to the fraction of the positive class (in this case, the fraudulent transactions). In order to plot a calibration plot, we use the following code:

```
#Extracting the probabilites that the positive class will be predicted

knn_proba = knn_classifier.predict_proba(X_test)
log_proba = logistic_regression.predict_proba(X_test)

#Storing probabilities in a list

probas = [knn_proba, log_proba]

# Storing the model names in a list

model_names = ["k_nn", "Logistic Regression"]

#Creating the calibration plot

skplt.metrics.plot_calibration_curve(y_test, probas, model_names)

plt.show()
```

This results in the following calibration plot:

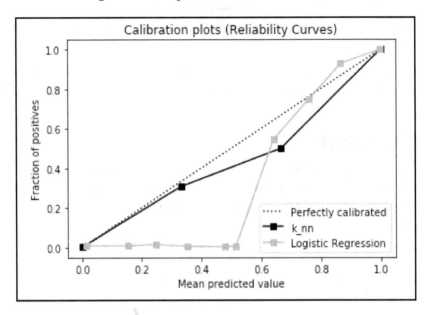

Calibration plot for the two models

In the preceding code, the following applies:

1. First, we compute the probability that the positive class (fraudulent transactions) will be predicted for each model.
2. Then, we store these probabilities and the model names in a list.
3. Finally, we use the `plot_calibration_curve()` function from the `scikit-plot` package with these probabilities, the test labels, and the model names, in order to create the calibration plot.

This results in the preceding calibration plot, which can be explained as follows:

- The dotted line represents the perfect calibration plot. This is because the mean prediction value has the exact value of the fraction of the positive class at each and every point.
- From the plot, it is clear that the k-nearest neighbors model is much better calibrated than the calibration plot of the logistic regression model.
- This is because the calibration plot of the k-nearest neighbors model follows that of the ideal calibration plot much more closely than the calibration plot of the logistic regression model.

Learning curve

A **learning curve** is a plot that compares how the training accuracy scores and the test accuracy scores vary as the number of samples/rows added to the data increases. In order to construct the learning curve for the k-nearest neighbors model, we use the following code:

```
skplt.estimators.plot_learning_curve(knn_classifier, features, target)

plt.show()
```

This results in the following plot:

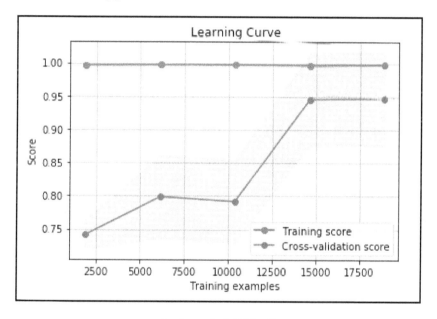

Learning curve for the K-NN model

In the preceding curve, the following applies:

1. The training score and the test score are only the highest when the number of samples is 15,000. This suggests that even if we had only 15,000 samples (instead of the 17,500), we would still get the best possible results.
2. Anything under the 15,000 samples will mean that the test cross-validated scores will be much lower than the training scores, suggesting that the model is overfit.

Cross-validated box plot

In this plot, we compare the cross-validated accuracy scores of multiple models by making use of box plots. In order to do so, we use the following code:

```
from sklearn import model_selection

#List of models

models = [('k-NN', knn_classifier), ('LR', logistic_regression)]

#Initializing empty lists in order to store the results
cv_scores = []
model_name_list = []

for name, model in models:
    #5-fold cross validation
    cv_5 = model_selection.KFold(n_splits= 5, random_state= 50)
    # Evaluating the accuracy scores
    cv_score = model_selection.cross_val_score(model, X_test, y_test, cv =
cv_5, scoring= 'accuracy')
    cv_scores.append(cv_score)
    model_name_list.append(name)
# Plotting the cross-validated box plot

fig = plt.figure()
fig.suptitle('Boxplot of 5-fold cross validated scores for all the models')
ax = fig.add_subplot(111)
plt.boxplot(cv_scores)
ax.set_xticklabels(model_name_list)
plt.show()
```

This results in the following plot:

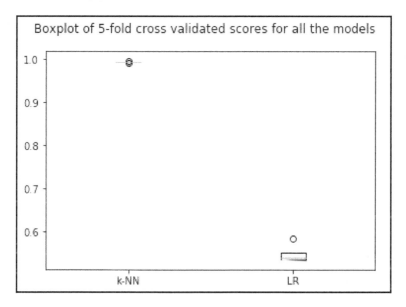

Cross-validated box plot

In the preceding code, the following applies:

1. First, we store the models that we want to compare in a list.
2. Then, we initialize two empty lists, in order to store the results of the cross-validated accuracy scores and the names of the models, so that we can use them later, in order to create the box plots.
3. We then iterate over each model in the list of models, and use the `model_selection.KFold()` function in order to split the data into a five-fold cross-validated set.
4. Next, we extract the five-fold cross-validated scores by using the `model_selection.cross_val_scores()` function and append the scores, along with the model names, into the lists that we initialized at the beginning of the code.
5. Finally, a box plot is created, displaying the cross-validated scores in a box plot.

The list that we created consists of the five cross-validated scores, along with the model names. A box plot takes these five scores for each model and computes the min, max, median, first, and third quartiles, in the form of a box plot.

In the preceding plot, the following applies:

1. It is clear that the K-NN model has the highest value of accuracy, with the lowest difference between the minimum and maximum values.
2. The logistic regression model, on the other hand, has the greatest difference between the minimum and maximum values, and has an outlier in its accuracy score, as well.

Performance evaluation for regression algorithms

There are three main metrics that you can use to evaluate the performance of the regression algorithm that you built, as follows:

- **Mean absolute error (MAE)**
- **Mean squared error (MSE)**
- **Root mean squared error (RMSE)**

In this section, you will learn what the three metrics are, how they work, and how you can implement them using scikit-learn. The first step is to build the linear regression algorithm. We can do this by using the following code:

```
## Building a simple linear regression model

#Reading in the dataset

df = pd.read_csv('fraud_prediction.csv')

#Define the feature and target arrays

feature = df['oldbalanceOrg'].values
target = df['amount'].values

#Initializing a linear regression model

linear_reg = linear_model.LinearRegression()

#Reshaping the array since we only have a single feature

feature = feature.reshape(-1, 1)
target = target.reshape(-1, 1)
```

```
#Fitting the model on the data

linear_reg.fit(feature, target)

predictions = linear_reg.predict(feature)
```

Mean absolute error

The mean absolute error is given by the following formula:

$$\frac{1}{n} \sum_{i=1}^{n} |y_i - \hat{y}_i|$$

MAE formula

In the preceding formula, y_i represents the true (or actual) value of the output, while the $\hat{y}_i$ hat represents the predicted output values. Therefore, by computing the summation of the difference between the true value and the predicted value of the output for each row in your data, and then dividing it by the total number of observations, you get the mean value of the absolute error.

In order to implement the MAE in scikit-learn, we use the following code:

```
from sklearn import metrics

metrics.mean_absolute_error(target, predictions)
```

In the preceding code, the `mean_absolute_error()` function from the `metrics` module in scikit-learn is used to compute the MAE. It takes in two arguments: the real/true output, which is the target, and the predictions, which are the predicted outputs.

Mean squared error

The mean squared error is given by the following formula:

$$\frac{1}{n} \sum_{i=1}^{n} (y_i - \hat{y}_i)^2$$

MSE formula

The preceding formula is similar to the formula that we saw for the mean absolute error, except that instead of computing the absolute difference between the true and predicted output values, we compute the square of the difference.

In order to implement the MSE in scikit-learn, we use the following code:

```
metrics.mean_squared_error(target, predictions)
```

We use the `mean_squared_error()` function from the `metrics` module, with the real/true output values and the predictions as arguments. The mean squared error is better at detecting larger errors, because we square the errors, instead of depending on only the difference.

Root mean squared error

The root mean squared error is given by the following formula:

$$\sqrt{\frac{1}{n}\sum_{i=1}^{n}(y_i - \hat{y}_i)^2}$$

The preceding formula is very similar to that of the mean squared error, except for the fact that we take the square root of the MSE formula.

In order to compute the RMSE in scikit-learn, we use the following code:

```
import numpy as np

np.sqrt(metrics.mean_squared_error(target, predictions))
```

In the preceding code, we use the `mean_squared_error()` function with the true/real output and the predictions, and then we take the square root of this answer by using the `np.sqrt()` function from the `numpy` package.

Compared to the MAE and the MSE, the RMSE is the best possible metric that you can use in order to evaluate the linear regression model, since this detects large errors and gives you the value in terms of the output units. The key takeaway from using any one of the three metrics is that the value that these `metrics` gives you should be as low as possible, indicating that the model has relatively low error values.

Performance evaluation for unsupervised algorithms

In this section, you will learn how to evaluate the performance of an unsupervised machine learning algorithm, such as the k-means algorithm. The first step is to build a simple k-means model. We can do so by using the following code:

```
#Reading in the dataset

df = pd.read_csv('fraud_prediction.csv')

#Dropping the target feature & the index

df = df.drop(['Unnamed: 0', 'isFraud'], axis = 1)

#Initializing K-means with 2 clusters

k_means = KMeans(n_clusters = 2)
```

Now that we have a simple k-means model with two clusters, we can proceed to evaluate the model's performance. The different visual performance charts that can be deployed are as follows:

- Elbow plot
- Silhouette analysis plot

In this section, you will learn how to create and interpret each of the preceding plots.

Elbow plot

In order to construct an elbow plot, we use the following code:

```
skplt.cluster.plot_elbow_curve(k_means, df, cluster_ranges=range(1, 20))
plt.show()
```

This results in the following plot:

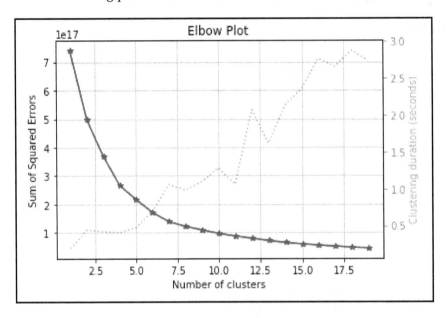

Elbow plot

The elbow plot is a plot between the number of clusters that the model takes into consideration along the *x* axis and the sum of the squared errors along the *y* axis.

In the preceding code, the following applies:

- We use the `plot_elbow_curve()` function with the k-means model, the data, and the number of clusters that we want to evaluate
- In this case, we define a range of 1 to 19 clusters

In the preceding plot, the following applies:

- It is clear that the elbow point, or the point at which the sum of the squared errors (*y* axis) starts decreasing very slowly, is where the number of clusters is 4.
- The plot also gives you another interesting metric on the *y* axis (right-hand side), which is the clustering duration (in seconds). This indicates the amount of time it took for the algorithm to create the clusters, in seconds.

Summary

In this chapter, you learned how to evaluate the performances of the three different types of machine learning algorithms: classification, regression, and unsupervised.

For the classification algorithms, you learned how to evaluate the performance of a model by using a series of visual techniques, such as the confusion matrix, normalized confusion matrix, area under the curve, K-S statistic plot, cumulative gains plot, lift curve, calibration plot, learning curve, and cross-validated box plot.

For the regression algorithms, you learned how to evaluate the performance of a model by using three metrics: the mean squared error, mean absolute error, and root mean squared error.

Finally, for the unsupervised machine learning algorithms, you learned how to evaluate the performance of a model by using the elbow plot.

Congratulations! You have now made it to the end of your machine learning journey with scikit-learn. You've made your way through eight chapters, which gave you the quickest entry point into the wonderful world of machine learning with one of the world's most popular machine learning frameworks: scikit-learn.

In this book, you learned about the following topics:

- What machine learning is (in a nutshell) and the different types and applications of machine learning
- Supervised machine learning algorithms, such as K-NN, logistic regression, Naive Bayes, support vector machines, and linear regression
- Unsupervised machine learning algorithms, such as the k-means algorithm
- Algorithms that can perform both classification and regression, such as decision trees, random forests, and gradient-boosted trees

I hope that you can make the best possible use of the application based on the knowledge that this book has given you, allowing you to solve many real-world problems by using machine learning as your tool!

Other Books You May Enjoy

If you enjoyed this book, you may be interested in these other books by Packt:

Python Machine Learning Blueprints - Second Edition
Alexander Combs

ISBN: 9781788994170

- Understand the Python data science stack and the algorithms in use
- Apply machine learning techniques to real-world applications
- Explore the power of Tensorflow and Keras using complex datasets
- Get up and running with topics like NLP, regression, classification, recommendation systems, and Bayesian techniques
- Learn to scale up a project using PySpark and build a chatbot
- Delve into advanced concepts like Computer Vision, Neural Networks and Deep learning

scikit-learn Cookbook
Trent Hauck

ISBN: 9781783989485

- Address algorithms of various levels of complexity and learn how to analyze data at the same time
- Handle common data problems such as feature extraction and missing data
- Understand how to evaluate your models against themselves and any other model
- Discover just enough math needed to learn how to think about the connections between various algorithms
- Customize the machine learning algorithm to fit your problem, and learn how to modify it when the situation calls for it
- Incorporate other packages from the Python ecosystem to munge and visualize your dataset

Leave a review - let other readers know what you think

Please share your thoughts on this book with others by leaving a review on the site that you bought it from. If you purchased the book from Amazon, please leave us an honest review on this book's Amazon page. This is vital so that other potential readers can see and use your unbiased opinion to make purchasing decisions, we can understand what our customers think about our products, and our authors can see your feedback on the title that they have worked with Packt to create. It will only take a few minutes of your time, but is valuable to other potential customers, our authors, and Packt. Thank you!

Index

www.ingramcontent.com/pod-product-compliance
Lightning Source LLC
Chambersburg PA
CBHW080532060326
40690CB00022B/5102